D1216068

Life's Journey of a Refugee

Fluvanna County Public Library
P.O. Box 548 Carysbrook
Fork Union, VA 23055

Life's Journey of a Refugee

◆

Memoirs of a World War II Survivor

Edwin Stalzer

iUniverse, Inc.
New York Lincoln Shanghai

Fluvanna County Public Library
P.O. Box 548 Carysbrook
Fork Union, VA 23055

Life's Journey of a Refugee
Memoirs of a World War II Survivor

All Rights Reserved © 2004 by Edwin Stalzer

No part of this book may be reproduced or transmitted in any form or by any means, graphic, electronic, or mechanical, including photocopying, recording, taping, or by any information storage retrieval system, without the written permission of the publisher.

iUniverse, Inc.

For information address:
iUniverse, Inc.
2021 Pine Lake Road, Suite 100
Lincoln, NE 68512
www.iuniverse.com

ISBN: 0-595-33426-1 (pbk)
ISBN: 0-595-66920-4 (cloth)

Printed in the United States of America

921
STALZER
8-25-05-9

Fluvanna County Public Library
P.O. Box 548 Carysbrook
Fork Union, VA 23055

*In loving memory of my parents, Rosa and Adolf Stalzer,
whose moral strength and integrity became my role model for life.*

Contents

Preface

Allied bombers over Yugoslavia in 1944

Preface

Down they came again, yet again, hundreds of Russian planes, hideous silhouettes jagged against a sky raging red with explosions above and apocalyptic fires below. A black monsoon of bombs flooded the town with debris, with panicked men and beasts in random flight, swarms of German soldiers dodging between buildings, maniacal antiaircraft and rifle fire, countless corpses blossoming in the devil's greenhouse.

The harder I ran, the faster I got nowhere. All around me lay friends mangled by explosives and collapsing buildings. They were beyond recognition and yet I knew them, could feel them beckoning me to relax in their inhuman bath. A nauseating wave of fear rolled my gaze upward as a building imploded into mass mayhem, revealing the flaming plane that had targeted me personally. Its malignancy pulsed the sky even brighter, psychotic orange. My frantic flight just pinned me closer to the bullseye. When its thunder and lightning crashed into me it seemed some other, baser creature was emitting the scream that pierced through the deafening roar to curl my skin, to burn the roots of my hair, to wake me up, wake up every refugee in the barracks.

Night sweat drenched my face and torso. My mother was bending over me, murmuring comfort, trying to help me up. It was some time before she once again became more real than the nightmare that had pitched me out of bed. Even her promise could not tempt me to resume my journey through the land of nightshade.

The same hallucination had haunted me for months. A dead man rose to shake my hand. I tried to run. He held me back. Sometimes he wore my father's face, sometimes no face at all. When I finally escaped it was with a bloody arm in my hand and howling laughter at my heels. Looking back, I saw his mangled shoulder regenerate the arm, and another arm and another, until the whole world was nothing but bloody arms lunging for my soul.

If the arms did not appear, the planes did. As soon as I dozed off they would come smashing in on me. Always dozens of bodies, sluices of blood. I was seven years old and I was a nervous wreck.

What I could not yet know was that my nightmare was a collective nightmare. It encapsulated the trials of an entire clan, of my ancestors, my people, the people of Gottschee, who set out in the early 14th century from an earlier Germanic Reich, in an earlier *Drang nach Osten*, carving settlements from the jungles of what is now Slovenia, near "Gottes See", the Lake of God, the Adriatic.

Not all the jungles were jungles to their Slav inhabitants, nor to Moslem raiders, and for six hundred years Gottscheers alternated peaceful coexistence with the tragedies of imperialism. They endured fire and sword, invasion and enslavement, reaching a spectacular climax at the fountainhead of modern ethnic cleansing.

The homeland they had forged was lost in the political jungle of twentieth-century Europe, but reclaimed throughout the world in numberless individual lives of horror, strength, faith and ultimate success. When we Gottscheers reunite on the first June Sunday in Franklin Square on Long Island, it is probably as the final generation, but also as the first regeneration, grateful for our assimilation and rebirth in open societies from America and Canada to Germany, Austria, even Australia.

Volumes have been written about the suffering of millions of people during World War II. Recognize all of the various nationalities, religious and ethnic groups. There were Poles, Russians, Hungarians, Lithuanians, Yugoslavians, Estonians, etc. Most of the books and movies that we are familiar with deal with the Holocaust.

There are few books and no movies dealing with the Catholic Land of Gottschee, a little linguistic island in the middle of the former Yugoslavia, who, after 600 years of living in relative harmony with the slavic population, suddenly became the subject of "ethnic cleansing" during World War II.

The subject of this book is the history of our people, and particularily my personal voyage and recollection of the events leading to the edge of extinction for this small group, our determination and perserverance, and ultimately, human triumph.

It is the mission of this book to present the reader with a true account of a story that begs to be told, in order to preserve the history of yet another ethnic group, a story that until now has only been told among the members of the group.

May the story you are about to read do its small part in the effort to help our children and grandchildren understand the price of their freedom, the struggles and ironic twists of history hidden behind the fortified city walls guarded by our patron Saint Bartholemew on the blue and white Gottschee coat of arms.

1

Heavy Turbulence 1918–1941

City of Gottschee as it looked through the centuries

Heavy Turbulence 1918–1941

Those were the turbulent and dangerous years, from the end of the First World War to the height of the Third Reich.

My grandparents, and my parents Rosa and Adolf, were descendants of Germans and had been able to live as Germans. But though the men of Gottschee did not fully understand the geopolitics, living as a German had meant fighting as a German, and losing the world war. The "linguistic island" of Gottschee was within the duchy of Carniola (Krain) in Austria, and the end of the Austro-Hungarian Empire was the beginning of the end for the island.

Gottschee had been Germanic well before Columbus landed in America. Rudolf von Habsburg had decided to settle the pristine forests between the Gurk and Kulpa rivers. Otto von Ortenburg's first Gottschee settlement in Moosbach dated all the way back to 1330 and the name "Gottschee" had first appeared in documents in 1363. By the time Holy Roman Emperor Friedrich II brought Gottschee into the House of Habsburg in 1456, the first church had been standing in Mooswald for more than a century. Gottschee had been an official "Regional Marketplace" for seventy years, and it had been thirty years since the last Count von Cilli had built Castle Friedrichstein.

Friedrich and his successors had rescued Gottschee after repeated catastrophic attacks. The Warlord of Bosnia had brought in his Turkish army to burn both town and church to the ground in 1469, carrying many off into the captivity and slavery that were to become the recurring Gottschee nightmare. Friedrich rebuilt Gottschee on the bank of the river Rinse and elevated it to the rank of city. This meant Gottschee had an official coat of arms, blue and white: a shield with fortifications for edges and a fortified house inside, Saint Bartholemew keeping watch in front with his white sword.

In 1471 Friedrich granted the city its freedom and in 1479 he exempted it from taxation within a six-mile radius. The Turks proceeded to decimate Gottschee again in 1480 and 1491, and to reverse the devastation Friedrich boosted economic and cultural recovery in 1492 by allowing Gottscheers freedom to trade both door-to-door and internationally. This privilege, rare in a feudal empire, fostered our distinctive traditional linens and woodcarvings.

Gottschee had meant Austria ever since, unless you count the strange blip from 1809 to 1815, when Polish enmity helped force Gottschee into Napoleon's "Illyria".

The Slavs did not forget or forgive German loyalties when the Empire broke up and Gottschee became part of the Kingdom of Yugoslavia. Suddenly

Gottscheers, who had lived in relative harmony with their immediate neighbors, became an ethnic minority in the Yugoslav state of Slovenia, surrounded by hostile Slavs. This tension was the seed of ethnic cleansing as we know it in today's Balkans.

True, my parents' generation was offered the option of 'returning' to Austria after the war, but not everyone could take advantage of it. Educated Gottscheers got out while the getting was good, to escape Slavification and put their training to use in the new Austria, but my family were farmers.

Farm children were hardly academics, but if they wanted to survive they learned a skilled trade to supplement their families' farm and timber income: natural agricultural talent was not enough to guarantee even food and clothing. My father had made himself into a most accomplished cooper. He built excellent bathtubs, barrels, butter churns, buckets—anything that held liquid. At the time these were bartered for flour, sugar, salt, clothing, tools and farm implements. Later they would become the salvation of our family.

Here I speak metaphorically. Gottscheers are devout Catholics, so their real salvation comes from faith, hope and love. Many of the happier anecdotes handed down through my family center on Church life: weddings, Confirmations, First Communions.

Religious devotion can have a terrible price. The Church of Bartholomaes outside Friedrich's original fortifications also symbolizes the Gottschee perspective on the central Christian theme of death and transfiguration, suffering and redemption. Over and over Gottschee churches were burned to the ground by invaders, and when a little girl set fire to the wooden city in 1596, even the church bells melted. They melted again in the fire of 1684, all eighteen tons of them. But the main altar remained standing, just as Saint Bartholemew remains standing at the forefront of our blue and white coat of arms. Whether we are struck by villainy, by accident, or by natural decay, the seed of renewal is always there in the ruins if you are willing to cultivate it.

Admittedly Gottscheers did also have a superstitious vein the Catholic Church would not endorse. Contact with Serbian and Croatian Gypsies had led them to fear witchcraft in particular. If you caught cold it was because a witch had crept in during the night and sat on your chest. When they told their kids not to come home through the woods at night because the witches were out, part of them really meant it.

This made the Grimms' fairy tale of Hänsel and Gretel supremely popular even in my day. Their dastardly stepmother decided to get rid of her pesky stepkids by leading them astray in the woods. Hänsel figured out he could fill his and his sister's pockets with pebbles and strew them to mark the way home. They made it back, but the stepmother made sure they had no pebbles the second time around. Hänsel tried to use bread crumbs instead, but the birds ate them. He and Gretel got lost, deeper and deeper in the forest, until they came upon a gingerbread house. No sooner had they reached for a piece than a wicked old witch dragged them inside and caged them, announcing she was going to fatten them up until they were ready to eat. Each day she demanded they stick their finger out of the cage to test their plumpness. But Hänsel had discovered she was blind, and bought them time by sticking out a piece of wood instead of a finger. One day they managed to outwit the old witch, throw her into her own oven and bake her. They found their way home and everyone lived happily ever after.

A pretty gruesome story to tell young children. Fortunately haute cuisine was not the only way to beat witches. Word was that if you carried a blessed crucifix at all times, indeed if you carried any object blessed by a priest, they couldn't touch you; so everyone carried a blessed cross. Would that this had been enough to neutralize the witches' brew of ethnic hatred.

The Slavs had taken over from the Austrians on the first day of 1919 and immediately set about purging all German officials and intellectuals. "Slavification" meant even German School Associations and clubs were outlawed. You were even supposed to call Gottschee by its Slovenian name, Kocevje.

Gottscheers had begun emigrating in 1879; by the time the worldwide Depression hit, there were more of them in the USA than in Gottschee itself. But some of those emigrants had always returned to enrich and expand Gottschee with their newfound wealth. The brain drain under Slavification was more like the decimation by war and enslavement in earlier centuries. The more educated got out to Austria and beyond while the getting was good, and Gottscheers in America got the message to stay put.

Those left behind were determined to resist persecution. They wanted to keep their traditional autonomy. The American melting pot was one thing, the Slovenian quite another. Gottscheers kept on teaching their children and conducting their services in their own language. The refusal to breed Slovenian speakers infuriated the Yugoslav authorities, and in 1921 they put the fix in, denying the Gottschee minority the right to vote. The city council became exclusively Slovenian.

Taking things lying down is not the Gottschee style. The Gottscheers formed the Gottscheer Agricultural Party to fight the theft of their voting rights. In 1924 they won 9 of the 16 seats on the City Council. In response the Slovenians just deepened the fix by upping the number of seats to 25 so the Gottscheers would stay in the minority.

With the death of the last Baron of Gottschee and the Slovenian confiscation of his enormous lands, the push was really on to turn all Gottscheers into Slavs. All able-bodied young men were drafted into the new Yugoslav army. My father's turn came in 1929, when he was 18.

The military command did not merely condone brutal beatings of Gottscheers, they positively encouraged them. Luckily they discovered my father's talent for riding and training horses, and put him in command of a Colonel's parade horses. This eventually meant special privileges, including protection from beatings.

My father often spoke proudly about the honor of riding the beautiful horses in parades, but his real pride was as a defiant Gottscheer. Young Gottscheers had started to make their Slav counterparts uneasy every time they rolled into town. The feud was destined to last for decades and eventually erupt into armed conflict, claiming many lives.

One night my father came face to face with some Slovenian partisans and heated words led to a barroom brawl with weapons drawn. He avoided getting stabbed and managed to inflict some head wounds with a whiskey bottle. Then someone punched him below his left eye and popped it right out of its socket. He claimed he never went to a doctor, just popped it back in with a white handkerchief; in a week it was good as new. Was he exaggerating? I have no idea, but the story certainly fit his character.

Gottscheers and Slavs came to blows even in church, since Gottscheers refused to pray in Slovenian. Gottscheer German was special. Isolation had kept it much more medieval than mainstream German, the same way independence has kept aspects of American pronunciation more Shakespearean than modern British. The more their linguistic identity was prohibited, the more Gottscheers rebelled. The Ljubljana government called it treason. Their strategic habit of prohibition ensured that my generation still speaks Gottscheer German today.

Their final insult was the decree that all Gottscheer schoolchildren simply be registered as Slavic. If their names could not be be translated directly into Slavic, the pronunciation and endings would be Slavicized. This let the bureaucrats make their Slavification quotas, at the cost of forcing many children to drop out of school.

Such was the atmosphere I was born into on the second day of May, 1939, with the Second World War just months away and 36000 Gottscheers virtually imprisoned by Slovenians, Croats and Serbs, all filled with hate and bent on destroying all Germans.

A diabolically apt moment for Hitler's Reichstag speech of October 6, 1939. With millions of German men lost in the world war, and millions more due to die in the years to come, he insisted Germany replenish the supply of "German blood" by relocating all of Europe's ethnic Germans into a redefined Reich. Never mind that the "German blood" in question was 600 years old and possibly tainted with "Slavic blood". Reichsführer SS Heinrich Himmler would take care of that little detail in his new role as "Imperial Commissioner for the Consolidation of the German People".

Germany and Italy set up Consolidation offices in South Tyrol, and to Gottscheers at the end of their ropes Nazification looked like homeland defense. Every village enthusiastically formed its unit of the "Gottscheer Mannschaft" or Gottschee Team, with a "Sturmführer" or Storm Leader at the helm. These teams were the backbone of the paramilitary that sought to protect Gottscheer civilians through preemptive attack on the Slovenian partisans. Every man from 18 to 50 was drafted.

At that moment Germany seemed likely to win the war. Enraging the Slovenians, Gottscheers cheered rumors of the German Army sweeping across Europe, and dreamed of liberation by the Wehrmacht infantry. The Gottscheer leadership had deluded itself into full-scale collusion with the Reich, complete with war songs and uniforms.

The bait in the devil's bargain was the hope that if the Yugoslavia of their tormentors were to fall, Gottscheers would not have to relocate. Little did the leadership realize that in 1941 the Reich was signing with Mussolini to conquer Yugoslavia, annex Southern Styria—and turn any remaining Gottscheers into Italian citizens.

The shocking truth came to light after Germany quickly vanquished the Kingdom of Yugoslavia that year. When the Gottscheer Mannschaft moved to disarm and replace the Slovenian police it became clear that the German army had orders not to advance beyond a predetermined line well short of Gottschee County. Much to the chagrin of Gottscheers, 'liberation' instead came courtesy of Mussolini's armies. Who in their turn wanted all the streets to have Italian names. There is just no end to ethnic chauvinism.

Decades later a kind of message in a bottle would wash up one day on the shores of my consciousness, from the sea of adult immersion in history and current affairs. It would explain why the curses I had heard from adults in those days made no sense: they were not German phrases but relics of Italian occupation.

Translated, they were even more obscene than they sounded, utterly unmention-able in these pages.

On my second birthday Gottschee officially accepted the inevitability of coop-eration with the Italian occupiers, handing the new Italian high commissioner a declaration of allegiance to Mussolini. Gottscheers did still have illusions enough to include a list of suggestions and wishes. These the Italians had no intention of even considering; they offered only the stark choice between Italian citizenship and relocation to the 'Reich'.

Our militarized leaders put a brave face on this, starting a campaign to con-vince us the inevitable relocation was a "return to the homeland". There had been no great pull towards the "homeland" over the previous 600 years, to be sure. But Hitler had declared us German citizens again and we were to be indoctrinated into the Reich. We were going "home to Germany".

Just not quite the Germany everyone had envisioned. Germany now meant the entire Reich, including German-annexed Yugoslavia. Forget the bright lights of Berlin, we were headed for Untersteiermark, Lower Styria.

Officially we were told that for leaving our farm, which had been in our family for generations, we would be compensated with an equally large farm in Lower Styria. We glimpsed the real shape of things to come in a leaflet circulated by the Yugoslavian Communist Party:

> **The Nazi leaders have resolved to resettle you on soil and farms they have stolen from Slovenian farmers. You will be considered thieves of these farms and will be driven out. We will set these farms on fire and will kill all of you.**

Gottscheers knew a train would be coming for them as it had come to relocate other ethnic Germans. On its side was painted the name "Heinrich". Himmler's final order on Gottschee resettlement came that October, 1941: we had one month to decide between staying in Italy or moving to the Reich in dead of a harsh winter.

Relocation was not going to be a joyride. The first train did not make it through for us until a week before the deadline and it could take only a fraction of the Gottscheers. It was followed by a convoy of seventy trucks, but the Dutch drivers refused to risk the partisan attacks inevitable on a journey through the for-est. The point was moot, since their fuel never arrived and snowdrifts had made the roads impassible. The remaining farm families, including ours, were finally forced to resort to horse-drawn wagons and sleds, hurriedly packed with provisions and whatever valuables we could cram in.

Later we found out that although the villages we had vacated were all destroyed by Tito's partisans, and although they burned down castle after castle, the German army had occupied and held the ruins of Auersberg Castle in late 1943 when Mussolini fell. In retrospect you can almost imagine it might have been better to stay put. Then you remember Father Joseph Eppich, the owner of the Gottscheer News, one of the very few who refused to leave. He ended up caught in the crossfire between the partisans and the Italians.

1941, resettlement, is my earliest childhood memory. I was about two and a half and my brother Richard, my only living sibling, five and a half. My recollection is too vague to single out everyone present on the exodus: my grandparents, all my uncles and aunts and numerous cousins. I remember them from later visits to their new homes, and of course from much later visits in the USA.

What stands out most is the bitter cold of the journey, numbing our hands and feet. I have a picture of arriving at a farm, people taking us in; an image of drinking scalding tea, my feet immersed in warm water to get rid of the frostbite. Years later I discovered that were it not for the kindness of those strangers the entire family would have frozen to death.

After days of seemingly endless snow, we arrived in the city of Königsberg, about eighteen miles from the Ranner Triangle, a 300-square-mile strip of land along the Sava and Scota rivers. Our new farm was just three miles from Königsberg, in the little village of Kerschdorf.

Here my parents discovered that the Communist leaflet had been true: 37000 Slovenians had indeed been run out of their homes. As the Königsberg authorities put it, they had been relocated into 'camps', making way for the Gottscheers. The truth was that they were not 'relocated' but interned. Cleansed. Their 'camps' were horrifying. There was no real plan to give them any compensation at all, much less their farms back. Obviously this was an outrageous and extremely inflammable situation.

Hitler's promise to us had been a fraud too. The Styrian farms were supposed to be at least as large and comfortable as those we had been forced from. Instead they turned out to be badly run down. And partially destroyed. And small. And stolen.

Some of the younger and the hardier Slovenian Styrians had been fortunate enough to escape. They had taken to the hills to wage partisan guerrilla war against the Germans and against the Gottscheers, who were after all usurping their lands. It is easy to understand why they began attacking our farms and killing many of our neighbors. Even so, at the time Gottscheers had no choice but to fight back. The German Army supplied them with weapons for daily search-and-destroy missions. Life became a vicious circle of constant fear.

2

This Land Is Your Land

My father, Adolf Stalzer in Wehrmacht uniform 1944

This Land Is Your Land

Like many Gottscheers, my father was not amused at having been resettled into the role of usurper. He had been promised clear title to a farm in Germany, not more blood feuding in Slovenia. More importantly, he wanted the rightful owners of the farm to know the truth, and set off to find them. They turned out to be in one of the nearby camps, and his fluent Slovenian helped him convince them he was sincerely appalled. He promised we would clear out as soon as they were freed to return. Meanwhile he would bring them plenty of the farm's produce each week, for as long as he could escape detection. He kept his promise and they swore they would never forget his kindness.

As if life were not complicated enough, some of our former neighbors turned up in Party uniforms. Back in the homeland their properties had been so small that their families sometimes begged extra food from my father. Now they had false patents of nobility, red armbands and swastikas. They were his bosses and would instruct him in fulfilling his production quotas. This absurd arrogance made him chase them off the farm more than once. In response came harsh official reprimands and finally the ultimate punishment: the draft. The capricious fate that had once forced my Gottscheer father into a Yugoslav uniform would end up disguising him as a Reich infantryman and shipping him off to the Russian front.

Those ultimate war years, 1941 to 1945, warped reality so severely that memory loses the usual semblance of linearity. The flashbacks climax in visions of American air raids, bombers strafing, dogfights high above us, death and mayhem in every direction. We had to take cover more and more often as the partisans grew bolder and began attacking in broad daylight, making roadside corpses a routine spectacle.

One day we witnessed an American pilot ejecting as his fighter was blown out of the sky. His parachute glided elegantly into a hopeless ambush. The German soldiers led him away into the unknowable.

Most war stories ended with this nagging question mark, but not all. Many years later, a world away, I fell into conversation about the war with one of my New York employees, and when the subject of air raids came up, he started peppering me with questions about exactly where we had lived. When I said Lower Styria he could scarcely contain himself. Here before me stood a US Air Force Bombardier who could pinpoint the exact date and time he had dropped bombs on me.

The memory he triggered was especially vivid. When the sirens went off that day, we were in Königsberg on our way to visit my grandparents at their small farm just outside the city. It was a mad dash to the shelter, with the bombs collapsing a whole row of buildings en route, debris rocketing in every direction. One shock wave was evil enough to pick me up and slam me off a wall into the pavement. I should have been one of the bodies littering the street. Instead we all escaped with minor injuries.

Experiences like this put a morbid twist on your sense of humor, and I could not resist: "Frank, do you realize what this will do to your career with this company—attempted murder of the CEO?"

We had a good laugh at this, and Frank had another surprise up his sleeve. As the end of the war drew near in 1945, the allies had begun dropping leaflets and even chocolate bars and pens from airplanes. The leaflets urged German soldiers to realize that all was lost, that the smartest course was to lay down their arms and ignore further orders. "Save yourself. The war will be over in a matter of days."

We children were told not to go near any of the American manna. Rumor had it that the food was poisoned and the pens booby-trapped. We kept our distance from the pens, but could not believe candy wrappers so colorful could conceal poison. Our reckless credulity was rewarded with not only some of the best chocolates we had ever tasted, but also bright foil to wrap walnuts for the Christmas tree. The only downside was stomachache from overindulgence.

To whom did we owe this pleasant indisposition? To Frank, the chocolate bombardier, whom I eventually promoted to warehouse manager.

At the time nothing could have seemed less likely. There were German soldiers everywhere, even in bunkers right behind my grandparents' farm. We saw a great horde of them at a Nazi rally, waving their flags in the wind, singing war songs between the blaring speeches. Even boys my age were there, dressed up in khaki, marching like puppets, singing the verses that had been drilled into them. Endless repeats of Deutschland, Deutschland über alles (Germany, Germany above all else). And more sinister forebodings:

Wir haben den Frieden gebrochen,	*We have violated the peace,*
Für uns gibt's kein Zurück.	*For us there is no turning back.*
Wir werden weiter marschieren,	*Onward we will march,*
Wenn alles in Scherben fällt,	*Even if everything is crashing to pieces around us,*

Denn heute gehört uns Deutschland,   *For today Germany is ours*

Und morgen die ganze Welt.   *And tomorrow the whole world.*

How do I still remember these songs? Simple: my teenage cousins Karl and Erwin got a kick out of standing me on a table and making me sing them at the top of my lungs. This was the climax of the conflict with the partisans, and the settlers were fighting as Germans. Everyone had to participate in the Reich somehow. They even sent students to do their national service as apprentices on the farm, including a particularly nice Austrian medical student named Theresa, "Tesi", from Graz. She really opened our eyes to the wide world outside the Untersteiermark.

If you have never tried to live a normal life under these circumstances you will have a hard time judging them fairly. This was war, and even in peacetime farm children are closer to the cruelty of Nature. Did you ever watch your grandmother slaughter a rooster? We did, one winter visit. She held his white wings and legs in one hand and placed his neck on the chopping block. It stretched out reflexively, making him seem amazingly cooperative. Down came her little ax and severed his head with a single stroke. Then came the real horror. His pure white body wrenched itself from her hand and flew off, spiraling, spattering circles of blood far into the virgin barnyard snow.

In a sense we were pretty hardened kids, but this was part of normal farm existence and still is. Animals are not born filleted. If you wanted to eat well, you killed them yourself. We were taught that was God's intent. Chickens, rabbits, pigs, lambs, pheasants, calves, even squirrels: all were there to provide us with meat.

This was one reason I idolized my cousin Karl. Karl had grown up with us because he had no father and his mother had emigrated to Ridgewood in New York. He was like an older brother to me. When he hit his late teens, my parents sent him to the city as a butcher's apprentice. On one of his eagerly anticipated visits he offered to show off his new skills and slaughter one of the pigs who lived off to the left of the house, next to the chicken coop.

Slopping the pigs meant sliding across through the unbelievable stench to replenish their swill. This did not inspire great affection for them. Nonetheless the slaughter proved truly gruesome. Hauling the pig from the pen, they tied its feet and placed it in a large trough. Karl slit its throat from ear to ear, yet for more than an hour it refused to die. Unless you have witnessed this nearly endless screaming and struggling, you have no idea what the expression "like a stuck pig" really means. At any rate, even as an apprentice Karl made superb sausages, bacon and hams. These were hung in our own smokehouse; when they were finally ready they tasted so great that I wanted to become a butcher just like Karl when I grew up.

Though too young to grasp the details, we knew that like everyone in the 15-25 age bracket Karl was also getting combat experience in the "homeland protection" squad, trying to stave off the daily partisan attacks. He decided to show us the fundamentals of bombmaking. Waiting until my father was safely out of the way in the fields, Karl ferreted out his cache of gunpowder and explosives. He drilled a hole in a gigantic tree stump out front, charged it, attached a fuse, lit it—and blew up the stump in his own face. Blood streamed from his nose and mouth as he bemoaned the loss of his vision. All we knew to do was fetch our parents, who sent him off to the hospital with a horse and buggy as ambulance. He made a full recovery and returned to his apprenticeship, but not without a major lecture and proper punishment from my father.

The rough stuff with the animals contributed to my reputation as a little terror. As soon as my mother saw my blond head disappearing she knew trouble was due any moment. My best buddy and partner in crime was Fritz, the neighbors' son. When he showed up at our place he often threw rocks at our German shepherd Rex, who lived on a chain out front. Twice he made Rex angry enough to burst the chain and go after him. When the police came we had to explain why Rex did not deserve to be shot. Really he was a remarkably loyal dog, and we were sad when some months later a poisonous snake bit him and my father had to shoot him after all. I will never forget the look on his face as he watched my father digging the hole he seemed to know was his grave.

Fritz's teenage neighbor Irma, whose parents were my godparents, spent many hours as our babysitter and ended up naming her first child after me. One day she was sitting outside the house with me on her lap and my dog Rex curled up at her feet. On an exceedingly frisky impulse I kicked his head. He woke up in a daze and bit back, nipping my leg and drawing a little blood, but when he realized it was me he was more shaken up than I was. When he came crawling up to lick my leg he had a sorry look in his eyes and it seemed he was crying.

Sometimes the animals gave us a dose of our own medicine. When I was about five I got to hold the chain on the lead cow during the evening herding. It slipped from my hand, and when I went to fish it out from under her she stepped right on my bare foot.

The horses were the most merciful. Cleaning the stables was not much better than slopping the pigs, not really suitable work for children age five or six, and my parents caught me rushing through it one day with a pitchfork. They told me to be grateful the horses were smarter than I was. When I poked around their legs, they could have hauled off and kicked me to death; instead they just danced aside. Likewise with my father's white mare. She was his prize riding horse, too gorgeous to pull a carriage. I decided to steal her for a bareback joyride and was having the time of my life until she cleared a ditch and sent me flying. She could have crushed me like a bug. Instead she maneuvered adroitly away and I walked off practically unharmed.

It was the wild animals who gave us the real run for our money. The forests were packed with wolves, bears and wild boars. My father more than once came home with a beautiful bearskin rug, but the wolves were too notoriously vicious for one man to take them on alone. The ranchers convened every week and finally came up with a trap ingenious enough to snare as many as a dozen wolves on a single night. First they penned sheep or goats in an inner ring. Then they built an outer ring with an extra yard of radius. The wolf entered the outer ring by throwing open a little gate, and circled all the way around the inner pen. When he got back to the starting point he tried to move the open gate back out of his way. This locked it into place. Since the outer ring was too narrow for him to turn around, and since there were spikes angled to jab him if he backed out, it was checkmate, with plenty of room left for the next customer. The next morning would find them helplessly ringed round their tantalizing prey, to be shot like fish in a barrel. Their furs fetched a handsome profit.

My insatiable curiosity about what makes things tick almost led me into a similar trap. We had one chicken that always vanished when it was due to lay an egg. Clearly this chicken was up to no good and belonged under surveillance. I observed it shuffling around the corner of the barn and disappearing through a hole in the wall, just wide enough for me to fit too: the perfect opportunity for a cub detective. In I went, hot on her trail, into a tunnel winding up through the hay. It grew too narrow for me to turn around, but it seemed headed for the loft, with its ladder I had so often climbed from the other side. I did indeed emerge in the open upper loft, just as the hen doubled back for a sneak attack. I had stumbled upon her nest, at least ten chicks. Intrusions like this make mother hens somewhat aggressive. Solving The Case of the Missing Eggs cost me some pretty nasty facial scratches.

You might have thought my brother Richard an exception to the harsh rules, since he was usually the passive yin to my active yang. Being three years older, he pulled his punches, both for my sake and to avoid being punished as a bully. Try facing sibling rivalry with one hand tied behind your back. He had to write off more than one punch along the way. One day during a game of tag I even pulled back a branch and let it fly back at him like a slingshot. It knocked him flat, out cold, putting the fear of God into me and sending me running and shouting across the fields in search of my parents: "Richard got hurt, Richard got hurt." The passive voice did not fool them; I got a hearty dose of punishment.

My mother had a favorite story about Richie and the hard-boiled eggs she packed with his school lunches. One day he complained, "Mama, could you please boil the eggs a little longer? They are always a little too hard."

One day even this easygoing character lost his cool. He had fashioned a small mobile fence for his rabbits, so that when they overgrazed one patch of clover he could easily move them en masse to another. One day a rabbit escaped during the move and he went ballistic, heaving it up and dashing it to the ground. The poor creature's back was broken, its legs pathetically dragging along behind. It became supper before its time, which was probably the merciful thing at that stage. There must have been something wicked in the air that day; Richie told me later that to his immediate regret and shock he had gone on to lose his temper with me and knock the wind out of me by whacking my spine.

As far as I know, the most spectacular animal accident had nothing to do with naughty boys. The regular carriage horses were hitched to a wagon in front of the house, right next to our well. A few dozen yards down the road, just before the barn, stood a gigantic oak tree. One day when we were loading the wagon, some occult force sent the horses off in a panic. They galloped past opposite sides of the oak tree, and when the wagon hitch and pole caught on the tree they collided and cracked their skulls, collapsing instantly. The prospect of their almost certain death caused an uproar. The farm hands were able to coax them back to life in the end, but there must have been brain damage; they were never quite the same again.

Lest you imagine my mischief was limited to the placid beasts, I hasten to assure you of my credentials in playing with matches. Fritz brought some over and asked me if I knew where there might be some hay or straw for a bonfire. Well, duh, how about the huge supply in the barn. Dragging some outside, we lit up and watched it catch: first just a flame, then a bonfire, then a malignant demon laughing its way up the barn wall. Richard returned from school in time to sound the alarm and save the farm, but not soon enough to save us from terror. Boy, were we in trouble. There was no choice but to hightail it out of there and hide out in the neighbor's stable, leaving my parents and the farm hands to quench the blaze.

After what seemed like hours, the dust and smell of the stable became unbearable and we crept out for some fresh air. My father was still on the warpath for us and we fell straight into his hands. He carried me home by my ears for our traditional punishment: baring your knees and kneeling on coarse gravel, right out front where they could keep an eye on you. In this case I was lucky it was gravel and not a quartered log with the jagged edges up.

I could have been back on my feet in minutes, just by begging for forgiveness and swearing never to do it again. But I was born way too stubborn to capitulate before the pain became unbearable. This turned the punishment cruel and unusual. If a parent tried it today they would probably need a lawyer. Not that it did not work. I can honestly say I never repeated any crime I had been punished for. Why should I, with so many new crimes to explore?

Nothing parents could dream up would be as tragic and senseless as the punishment that awaited Fritz. He and I loved to climb cherry trees and stuff ourselves to the bursting point. I could never understand why, but Fritz generally declined to spit out the pits. The day finally came when he doubled over with pain. During the seven-mile journey to the hospital his appendix ruptured, and he was dead on arrival. No more than seven years old. The funeral is permanently etched on my memory, and now that I am a father myself I can begin to imagine the pain his parents must have felt.

So let us leave violent deeds and confession behind for the present, and turn to the moments of pure happiness. The most intense were the Christmas holidays, the freshly cut tree bedecked with edible ornaments: butter-cookie angels, birds, Christmas trees, animals. On the larger branches were fruits and candy: oranges, apples, pears, also walnuts, some of them nestled in bright foil like the wrappers rained on us by the chocolate bombardier. All the candles were real and everyone had to be present for the lighting ceremony. Christmas Eve meant riding off to midnight mass together in a horse-drawn sleigh; then a wonderful meal, with an extra magic dessert from the tree.

Holidays added a special overtone to the cozy heat spread through much of the house by the Kachelofen, the traditional glass-tiled stove occupying a whole corner of the kitchen. The Kachelofen did not just heat the house, it baked our daily bread and cured our meats with its chimney vent up above in the smokehouse. Most winter nights were spent around the bench running along its 7-foot sides, and—except for the night I fell off and broke my arm—it was the last word in comfort and security.

New Year's Eve was a special tradition that had united Gottscheers for 600 years. While the whole family sat in the Stube, the living room, singing and drinking tea in the snug warmth of the Kachelofen, neighbors would suddenly burst through the front door with large baskets. Everyone knew what was coming, but pretending to be surprised was half the fun. While we all shouted "Happy New Year", they threw delicacies into the middle of the room and the children scrambled for them. At some point in the evening our parents would go off to reciprocate.

The other great festival was harvest time. Of course, since food was plentiful, in one sense every day was a harvest day. Every morning we helped our mother gather fresh eggs; you never forget the taste of fresh eggs straight from the nest, fried in homemade butter, with homemade ham and home-baked bread. If we wanted milk we just went and milked a cow, or a goat. If we wanted cheese, we just went and made some. All sorts of fruit was ours for the plucking. But the full harvest brought in lots of extra hands and set the whole farm buzzing. We gathered wheat and corn, potatoes and fruit, turned grapes into wine and jam, all accompanied by musicians who turned work into a fabulous party.

The party was well and truly over in 1944, when Karl and my father each received induction notices from the German army.

Karl they sent as a mountain ranger to the American front, where he was wounded, captured and interned at an American prison camp in Munich. After a year they released him and permitted him to join his mother as a US citizen. But it was not yet time for the happy ending. Scarcely had he begun to put down roots when he was drafted into the US army, serving more than two years in Korea. He saved six of his buddies, despite himself having stepped on an anti-personnel mine, and was decorated and promoted to Sergeant after eighteen months recuperating in Japan. Finally he returned to Ridgewood and married a Gottscheer girl. He was to remain in New York, in Middle Village, the father of two sons and a daughter, and grandfather of four. But his son inherited the military globetrotting. He met his wife in a Catholic Church in Thailand and still serves the United States of America. They live outside Washington, DC with their two beautiful children.

For my father induction meant the Wehrmacht. He came home a few times during basic training, in his fancy uniform. But the visits soon stopped. They told us he had gone to Russia, riding lead in a team of six or so horses transporting cannons to the front lines. My mother had a few letters from the front, then he was gone. We pictured him fallen at Stalingrad.

War had robbed my mother of her husband and nephew, leaving her to manage a farm with two children and aged grandparents. The partisans were determined to be rid of the intruders and had crossed the line into outright ethnic cleansing. They moved in groups of twenty or more. Every day came fresh attacks and fresh atrocity stories. They had dragged Fritz's father from his house, pierced him with nails and dragged him again behind a horse until there was nothing left but gore; then they had burned his house down with the rest of his family inside. They had forced a young Gottscheer teacher to dig his own grave before bludgeoning him to death and tossing him in.

Many years later I still flashed on such episodes whenever I saw Indians massacring whites in Westerns. They might as well have been Slovenians, slaughtering Gottscheers like animals.

We knew our turn had come one night when we heard horses galloping around our house. All night we listened to their infernal circling as we hid beneath the living room table in terror. Come morning it grew quieter and we ventured out, only to discover that the horses we had heard were our own. Something had released them from the barn and spooked them into an endless gallop around the house. A false attack had thrown the true attackers off the scent.

It would be years before we fully accepted the only possible reason we could have been spared. We knew the sons of our farm's true owners were in the partisan army. What we could not know for sure was that despite the seductions of ethnic rage, their parents had been impressed enough by my father's kindness, and influential enough, to demonstrate an equally strong sense of justice. The triumph of honesty is sometimes scarcely imaginable in this sinful world, but nothing else could account for our safety; we were no less vulnerable than any other Gottscheers, and our men were known to have been drafted by the Reich.

Which was losing the war. The news from the front was harrowing. We had to prepare to abandon the farm and gamble on a desperate retreat to Austria.

3

Racing Against Extinction

Picture of a typical wagon used for flight out of Slovenia

Racing Against Extinction

Every Gottscheer could see the writing on the wall: the partisans would kill every one of us as soon as Germany withdrew from Slovenia.

The Reich was collapsing. Most of it was already occupied by the allies. Tito's partisans were inches from total control of the Yugoslavian countryside. Escape was now or never, yet there were no orders from Graz, not a peep. The authorities mutely maintained the mad pretense of normality as we watched the burning fuse chase down to the explosive end of Gottschee history.

May was the fateful month. During the first week a few hundred Gottscheers were evacuated to Austria by train. On May 8 came the final order for all of Gottschee to move. It was one of the last acts of the Third Reich, for that was the day Germany capitulated.

For days the Ranner Triangle had been a chaotic buzz of preparations for flight. The partisans attacked at will, intoxicated with their advantage, eager to press it home with maximum terror. The soundtrack was constant sniper fire, desperate German rear guard actions. The final mass meeting in Ran resolved that each family pack a horse-drawn wagon and await the signal from the leadership.

German soldiers were still ubiquitous, feigning an impossible security. Some of them looked shockingly childlike; Germany had run out of men and begun drafting boys, often too young even to carry their heavy machine guns and ammo. On every farm you could see people scurrying, hauling, loading, gathering animals. The urgency intensified constantly. We were down to the wire, invasion was imminent. The one gleam of hope was the German army's assurance of a Wehrmacht company to assure safe passage.

My mother lamented ignoring my father's final message that the war was lost and we should save ourselves immediately. This was the only lament we were to hear from her. Her incredible strength, faith and survival instincts were to carry all of us through seven brutal years as refugees.

Mama spent the remaining days cooking and baking, filling endless barrels of food. Only one wagon was allowed per family, so she chose the largest, with the strongest pair of horses, packing every inch until she thought we could make it to Austria: bread, milk, wine, potatoes, flour, huge smoked hams and sausages, cookies, even a few cows tied to the wagon.

When the day came, Main Street in Königsberg turned into a massive wagon train, stretching block after block, with parents at the reins and children ordered inside for relative safety from the inevitable partisan attacks. Had it not been for the heavily armed German soldiers guarding on every side, you might have thought yourself in the American West, though when the command came to move it was hardly as entertaining as "head 'em up, move 'em out".

The caravan wound its way through the streets of Königsberg, down a hill, around some tight curves, onto the open road. Another procession was leaving Rann at the same moment. There were wagons as far as the eye could see, which was not all that far given the dust swirling up from the unpaved highway.

Slovenian citizens lined the shoulder, cheering and catcalling with delight at our departure. These were our neighbors. For years they had feigned sympathy for us by day and donned their partisan uniforms by night. Now they could reclaim their farms and cast aside the burden of hypocrisy. I can't blame them for feeling giddy with their sudden freedom. How could Hitler have failed to see what he was setting us up for?

The descent from orderly departure to refugee nightmare was presaged by the young guard assigned to our wagon. Even now I need only close my eyes to see him in full detail: blond, blue eyes, medium build, sweat streaming down his face as he trudged along with his enormous machine gun. My mother kept telling him to rest it on the tailgate and he kept responding it was verboten. Refreshments, however, were not verboten and we made sure he had plenty.

The first few uneventful days lulled us into a false sense of security. Did we not have food and drink, and a kind of roof over our heads, and a security detail? As Königsberg faded far into the distance we allowed ourselves the fatal luxury of relief and optimism. Things would sort themselves out in Austria. People would welcome their lost cousins with open arms. Were we not Austrians, albeit 600 years removed? We needed only arrive quickly and in one piece.

Each passing mile brought more evidence of retreating armies: mountains of guns and ammunition, burned-out tanks and automobiles. Things had taken an ominous turn, yet we pressed on, halting at sunset to make our fires and cook our meals within the security perimeter. Except for the uneasiness we looked like a boy scout convention.

And some of us acted like one. The older boys had discovered the fascination of German hand grenades. They looked like potato mashers with a flashlight handle. You unscrewed the top to reveal a little blue knob attached to a fuse. After you pulled it you had five seconds or less to get rid of it. Toss it into the river and guess what floats to the surface.

That night we were enjoying the grenade fish over an open fire when disaster almost sent us too belly up. Some fiend managed to lob a live artillery shell into the fire. Kids went flying in the deafening blast. Pandemonium: children screaming in agony, parents crying, the grisly action painting of real blood. Though quite close to the fire, I managed not to join the many seriously injured. My brother Richard was not so lucky; he still bears the scars on the tops of his feet. This is the scene my mind conjures forth when I hear of suicide bombings in Israel, with army medics and parents scrambling to patch everyone up.

Throughout that night there were sporadic bursts of machine gun fire outside the encampment. The adults and soldiers who ventured out at daylight to investigate were shocked to discover a hastily covered mass grave. Even the children got word and sneaked over to witness the ultimate horror: arms protruding from the ground. Still moving.

Partisans had infiltrated the wagon train and dragged people into the woods for execution. Is it any wonder that children had nightmares for months and years thereafter? How should the mind ever dislodge such a scene?

One violent night had dispelled the illusion of a casual trip to safe harbor. The partisans were stalking us. They meant murder. The welcoming committee for a holiday in hell.

The next morning, Mama announced she and some other Gottscheer women were going to venture over to a local farm to ask permission to bake some fresh bread. She would be back well before it was time for the wagon train to move on. In retrospect this was obviously a foolish move. Naturally they were still gone when the order came to roll out. We frantically pleaded with the soldiers to wait for our missing mothers, but they would brook no discussion; the area was too dangerous to dawdle a single extra minute. To a child this was as traumatic as hearing you would never see your mother again.

The boy with the machine gun was still guarding our wagon and tried to assure us the ladies would hurry to catch up with us as soon as they saw the train leaving. We were too hysterical for this to be any comfort as the wheels started rolling. The only saving grace was that the wagons rolled so slowly, no faster than the soldiers guarding them on foot.

After what seemed like hours, our mother did finally come running up behind us. Catching up had meant jettisoning most of her bread, but we were far too overjoyed to care. She never left our side again.

The road led on through a deep valley, winding along a river between steep hillsides. Never was there a more perfect spot for an ambush; it was the wolf trap all over again, with no escape from the ravine and no turning back. People spotted the trap as soon as we entered it, gesturing up to the tops of the ridges. Fear gripped us when we realised they were lined with partisans on horseback. The soldiers prepared to fight even as they urged us to keep moving.

The first Allied fighter planes rolled in around noon. It was a dry run, not one shot; perhaps they were trying to panic the civilians out of the wagons into the ditches. The Wehrmacht opened up with machine gun and rifle fire, and we did head for the ditches, some for the shallows of the river, once the strafing began in good earnest. Half an hour of it seemed like half a normal day.

Silence returned, signaling the partisans to swarm in and surround us on all sides. They rode up and down the line, shouting and firing. They did not yet harm any civilian, but by the time they were done not one soldier was left alive. Behind our wagon lay our blond boy in a pool of blood, half his head blown off.

Victory shouts and loud orders drove it home. We were truly refugees, delivered into the hands of the Slovenian, Croatian and Serbian partisans.

Herding us into a big meadow running up the ridge, they stripped us of all our possessions, confiscating even the horses. We watched them gorging themselves on our smoked hams, sausages and bread, taking particular delight in our sugar cookies. They helped themselves to our women and young girls. They frolicked and held mock tugs of war over bits of booty. Gottscheers were left with nothing but the clothes on their back, and if they were really lucky, their lives too.

The next leg of the journey was a forced march, guarded by partisans on horseback. Our horses, as often as not. It didn't take too many guns to intimidate a crowd of women, children and the helpless elderly. The scene would have made quite an aerial shot, a major roundup.

One day's solid marching brought us out of the valley and into a large open area enclosed with high barbed wire. We were exhausted, feet blistered, the children crying uncontrollably.

For the partisans the operation had been a brilliant success, flawlessly planned and executed in perfect synch with the Allies. The Germans had to have known what awaited us in that valley. They must have been forced to gamble on making it through the only open passage.

Hundreds, perhaps thousands of weary refugees sank to the ground, dazed by the new developments. Would we ever get out of this alive, or were they just going to massacre us as they had always promised? They certainly looked menacing enough, waving their guns and firing into the air. And we had just seen them killing civilians in the final crossfire.

Loudspeakers began to blare partisan orders. Empty your pockets and bags, place everything on the ground in front of you. This scene was repeating itself all over the country, wherever wagon trains had headed for Austria.

As they searched us we heard a shot. One of the Gottscheer adults had been rash enough to conceal a German flag on his person; a partisan had shot him dead in a paroxysm of anger and disgust. Another dozen or so joined him in fastening it atop a pole and setting it aflame. This was distilled hatred, a desperately dangerous situation. Terrified Gottscheers produced piles of valuables, which the partisans wasted no time scooping into booty bags.

My grandfather was one of the first they searched. He had emptied his pockets as ordered, into a neat little pile: pocketwatch, penknife, tobacco pouch, wedding ring and so forth. But when they double-checked they found he had overlooked some cigarette papers in his shirt pocket.

An innocent holdout—men rolled their own smokes in those days—but it enraged the partisans. One of them gunwhipped Grandpa repeatedly across the face, spurting blood from his mouth and leaving deep gashes. He was still attacking as Grandpa collapsed. Had he not been pulled away by a more cool-headed officer, Grandpa might not have been able to continue the march with us a few days later.

Horrified by this scene, everyone scrambled to rid their pockets of every last dust mote. My mother went wild, wrenching my jacket and Richard's off our backs and ripping the sleeves right off them. Out flew a blizzard of paper money. She had had the foresight to sew it into the fabric, hoping we would at least have food money when we arrived; but with the war over the Reichsmark was now as worthless as the Confederate dollar.

You can imagine her sensations when her search of yours truly, age six, yielded a fully loaded .22 caliber semiautomatic pistol. This was not misguided macho, just a souvenir picked up along the journey, where retreating soldiers had lost or thrown away so many weapons that you could find anything you wanted. But the distinction would not have greatly interested the partisans. Mama had the great presence of mind frantically to dig a hole and bury the gun before a debate could begin. They found nothing and no one got hurt.

During the night there was more shouting and gunfire, and the next day more men were missing, executed on suspicion of Nazi party membership. Any possible resistance on our part was now completely shattered. This was it. Before it was over they would find some pretext to kill us all.

There was no food or water left and the partisans obviously had no intention of providing either, but since the perimeter was secure they let us mill about, even forage. There were puddles of rainwater we could both drink and use to boil grass or clover soup. Eventually we even came across a pile of potatoes. Spiteful partisans had turned these into a revolting sewer. Yet with survival at stake people eagerly quarreled over them, happy to rinse them off and boil them. The survival instinct also kindly protected us from the toxic realization that these were merely the symbolic hors d'oeuvres in a feast of evil.

Partisan anger appeared to lull as the first days went by. We imagined passion might be partly yielding to reason. By then they would also have been in contact with the Russians. There would be directives concerning refugees. Refugee massacres are not the best PR. The partisans were still pretty brutal, but the random killings stopped and things settled into an anxious limbo, a dream state. Amid the chronic hunger and thirst appeared a tentative sprout of hope. Yet we had lost too many illusions to forget the rumors of other groups completely wiped out by the partisans. This could well be nothing more than the calm before the storm. To underline the point there were occasional mass beatings, warnings against plotting for escape or rebellion—as if anyone had the strength even to think of fighting back. Further to intimidate us, they would fire shots into the air and glare at us so menacingly that we taught ourselves to avoid their gaze altogether for fear of provoking them.

Even in a war zone one never quite ceases to be amazed at complete disregard for human life. Everyone has heard of the Nazis, but fewer people realize that Slovenians, Serbs and Croats were also capable of world-class cruelty. The many stories gave us good reason to fear for our lives. The Serbs were reputed the most brutal, known to plunge knives into their victims while laughing in their faces. The Croatians were a close second. More of the Slovenians were simply displaced farmers forced into the fray when the Germans invaded Yugoslavia and carted their parents off to prison camps. The kids fled into the mountains and became guerrillas.

Some of them turned out to be pretty gentle people; in fact, one of them had taught me a deep lesson about how all men are created equal. I was standing by the roadside when a group of partisans walked by, temporarily out of strict formation. As he walked by me, his eyes fixed elsewhere, one young soldier handed me a piece of bread and an apple. His superiors might have beaten him for it, or worse, but he did not care. He did not see an enemy, just a starving kid.

Eventually lineups were ordered and it became clear that we were to be uprooted again. We left the encampment on foot, flanked by partisans on horseback. At the time we did not realize just how close we were to the Austrian border—we turned out to have hiked past Marburg, just south of Styria, southernmost Austria. We asked ourselves and the elders in disbelief: was it possible that they were going to let us leave Slovenia alive? If so, why did they bother to chaperone us? Did they not realize how desperate we were to leave immediately? If they intended to let us go, why did they act just as vicious and threatening as ever? The elders debated but there was just insufficient data.

Later, when the world learned more about that terrible time, it would hear of other Gottscheers who shared our wretched fate, and worse. Otterstädt recalls:

> They spent the first night in houses, in ruins, and outdoors in Lichtenwald, a village insignificant in itself, now filled with refugees and damaged by English air raids. The partisans guarded them from the edge of the village. By morning, they left the burning village of Lichtenwald and headed for Steinbrück under the guard of mostly adolescents. Repeated "luggage checks" en route saw to it that the Gottscheers first lost their vehicles, then their bundles, and finally their handbags, and when they finally reached the camp of Sterntal, also their money, jewelry, rings and identification papers. After days of murdering, cruel tortures, plundering, and inhuman sadism, the survivors arrived in the notorious camp of Sterntal near Pettau by way of Tüffer, Cilli, back again to Tüffer, and again to Cilli.

Survivors described Sterntal as a living hell. It was a former munitions plant with almost no sanitation. The thousands housed there suffered epidemics, hunger, maltreatment and murder. It was the final destination for hundreds of Gottscheers. Not one child under the age of two survived, including my infant cousin. Only the eventual intervention of the Red Cross halted the devastation.

We too were guarded by teenage partisans, eager to prove their manhood using the machine guns slung over their callow shoulders. Some of them had as much trouble carrying their weapons as our erstwhile blond guard.

It must have been right at the Austrian border that the partisans vanished like ghosts and the dreamscape shifted into a new war zone. This time it was the aftermath of an apocalyptic confrontation between the Russians and those Germans who refused to surrender. Complete chaos. Burning buildings, tanks and trucks in flames, smoldering equipment, everywhere the uniformed cadavers of Nazi storm troopers. Flares illuminated the dark sky and the ground below like fireworks. One of them landed on my grandfather's hand and burned him severely. Spontaneous bursts of gunfire seemed to celebrate the victorious Russian officer directing the lunatic proceedings, shouting orders from his white horse.

A hysterical Gottscheer mother came running up to him, yanking at his boots, frantically gesticulating at a farmhouse. A flash of understanding crossed his face; quickly dismounting, he raced into the house, down to the basement below, reemerging with half a dozen or more soldiers and a little girl, no more than twelve years old, crazy with screaming tears.

The Russian lined the men up in front of the farmhouse, took out his grease gun and shot them all dead before our eyes. At that instant I felt only yet another incomprehensible wave of violence. It would be years before I grasped that I had witnessed a righteous officer of the Russian army refusing to tolerate the enormity of child rape. It goes to show: virtue and vice are everywhere; no society can ever achieve a monopoly on either.

4

Camp 5

Catholic Church in Camp #5, viewed between two barracks

Camp 5

Little remained of the large group that had set out with such high hopes from Königsberg. Those spared by hunger and thirst had fallen prey to the partisans. A few had made their escape alone. The rest of us had dwindled to a ragtag band of two hundred or so. Both partisans and Russians had suddenly left to our own devices. We sought directions to the border, only to find we had already crossed into the presumed safety of Austria.

Our first stop was our first refugee camp: Spielfeld, barely outside Slovenia. It must have been Russian, since their army was occupying southern Styria, the Steiermark.

Here we had our first delousing with the insecticide DDT. Forced to undress, then powdered from head to toe, we came out looking like ghosts. We were to become exceedingly familiar with DDT, which was eventually banned in the USA as a toxic monstrosity. In my case it also seems to have worked pretty fast as a hair remover.

Delousing was our first taste of the endless hours refugees spend standing in line. Next was the communal shower. Now we were clean, disinfected, freezing and starving. They gave us a blanket and a berth: each of the large one-room barracks contained several dozen double-decker metal bunk beds and hordes of vermin. Apparently it had not occurred to them to use DDT on the roaches, bedbugs and mice.

Finally they lined us up before a large vat, handing us each a piece of bread and an empty army rations tin to be ladled full of a profoundly anonymous and suspicious fluid. Starvation is a great cook, so we devoured it regardless of smell and taste. That night we slept in a bed for the first time in weeks, still full of misgivings about the Russians' intentions, but mercifully exempt from beatings and shooting threats.

After a few days it became obvious we were not under detention, and some of us decided to resume our odyssey, further into the Styrian interior, as far as the small refugee camp at Wagna. Once again DDT, bunk, grub, rest and back on the road. The next camp, at Leibniz, was a decided step up: my grandparents were accepted as permanent residents, and we set them up in their barracks before moving on.

My mother clearly had a plan, something to do with Graz, the capital of Styria. To get there we spent nights at the side of the road, in stables, barns, burned-out farmhouses, eating whatever we could find as we made our way past Kirchbach and Hausmannstätten. By the time we arrived we had walked most of a 300-mile journey. Graz is nowhere near that far from Königsberg, so the road through captivity must have circled many detours.

My mother revealed she was searching for Tesi, the medical student who had worked for us in Kerschdorf. Tesi had in fact invited us to visit if ever we were in Graz. She had written down her address, and my mother had not only remembered it but protected it through repeated searches.

Finding Tesi was no small challenge with Graz under heavy Russian occupation and half the houses and buildings in ruins from Allied air raids. I still don't know how Mama managed it. In just a few days we were walking into an apartment building, up two flights of stairs, to a jubilant reunion. Tesi could hardly believe we had survived and were standing before her in the flesh. She asked after our father and was sad at the news.

Tesi was now a doctor, and married. Her two-room apartment was much too small for an extra family, but to help with food she gave us what little money she could spare, and she led us to the main refugee center. This was a large multistory building that might once have been a hospital or school, perhaps also a temporary barracks. They were processing hundreds of refugee applications a day, finding people slots in camps throughout Austria.

We were assigned beds in a large room with many other families. By this time we knew enough to hold our breath, pinch our nostrils and keep our eyes closed during our DDT dusting. The center was relatively comfortable and cheery, with two meals a day. They even introduced us to sugared teabags, a great luxury since sugar was so scarce. We ate them. Not bad.

The stress came at night, when Russian soldiers often crept into the rooms and into bed with girls, even married women. At first no one dared complain, but eventually word reached the administration and the Russian brass cracked down. Some briefly disobeyed the strict orders but soon they too thought better of it.

From our little island of security we could venture out into Graz, and we paid our visit to its perennial symbol, the Turm: a white, rectangular tower atop a steep hill at the center of the city, with a large clock on each of its four sides and a little mountain train for those who prefer not to climb the series of paths and stairs.

My mother grew fairly close to a Hungarian man we called "Mallaga", friend. He brought us sliced bacon and sausages and we were disappointed when he inexplicably slid out of our lives.

Russian grunts were busy looting homes abandoned at the unbearable peak of the air raids; many of the owners had disappeared or died, leaving most of their worldly goods behind. One day we were out walking, hoping to salvage some things for ourselves from the rubble, when we came to a public square full of loud Russians. Each had a burlap bag slung over his shoulder, bulging with ill-gotten gains. Suddenly one soldier's bag sounded a burglar alarm. He was so startled and frightened that he hurled it to the ground and riddled it with bullets. His comrades doubled over with laughter, seeing it was only an alarm clock; this angered him to the point of threatening them too with his gun.

When the center found us a slot it was at Lager #5, Camp 5, still in Styria, between Kapfenberg and Marein. On the appointed day we packed up our meager belongings and climbed onto the army truck for the half-hour ride to the train station. What met us there was disheartening: not a passenger train with the usual seats and windows, but a cattle train, the sort later made famous in movies about the concentration camps. The cars were unbearably hot, standing room only, packed like sardines. No water, no oxygen. Women and children were bawling. When the train lurched from the platform it crushed the crowd into the rear wall. Not until we were moving did settling allow some of us to slump to the floor.

On a globe our journey looks almost too short to mention, but these were the longest 100 miles I ever traveled. We stopped repeatedly to cram in even more refugees. At Bruck an der Mur they announced we were almost there. Then Kapfenberg, then the little village of Marein, where we could escape into open trucks for the final leg to the main gate of Camp 5, near the village of Pötschach.

If the walls of Camp 5 could speak, they would have quite a few dazzling tales to tell. The two hundred or so barracks had originally gone up to house construction workers for the munitions factory, producing cannons and anti-aircraft guns amid endless Allied raids. After the war the complex became an Allied debriefing center for German and Austrian POWs on their way home. The Russian occupation force took it over very briefly in August 1945, building observation and machine gun towers for a POW camp of their own. Then came a new agreement with the Allies and a changing of the guard. The British took over the entire province of Styria including the camp, which they changed into their branch of the United States Escapee Program.

By the time we got there it had changed into a refugee compound. The barbed wire atop the high chain link fence made it look like a prison camp. Home sweet home. The gate swung open and in we rolled, unloading at yet another processing center, for yet another series of lines, another DDT stripdown. This time it was much kinder and gentler: the nurses actually seemed to care. When the barracks assignment came we knew it would probably be the last and longest stop before our assimilation into the Austrian economy. What we did not yet know was how alien we ethnic Germans seemed to the impoverished Austrians. We were not brothers but distant Hungarian, Czech and Gottscheer cousins, economic rivals, 5000 new mouths to feed in this camp alone.

With numbers like those you need rules and regulations, and the British proved superb administrators, crafting a miniature self-governing community. Each barracks was broken down into blocks; interviewers probed the skills of each refugee and assigned him or her appropriate block duties, with the block leaders reporting to the military commander. They allowed the refugees to draft their own police force and maintenance crew. They ran an efficient infirmary and a camp school, staffed initially with educated refugees and later with Austrian teachers.

Since the community was not yet producing any marketable product, trade was still out of the question and all food had to be trucked in courtesy of the British. It tasted as you would expect from a military kitchen, but it was three square meals a day, quite a change from recent months. A modicum of stability had returned to our lives. There was even a barracks set aside as a Roman church for the many devout Catholics among us. For the first time we could recall, no one was out to kill us. From the ashes of fear and despair grew hope, determination to persevere in this alien environment.

Our barracks was close to the main gate. It was a rectangular room with windows along the long sides and a potbelly stove in the center, towards the front door. A dozen or so double-decker metal bunks stood in neat rows. The mattresses were soiled, but we each got clean sheets and a pillow with a coarse, striped pillowcase. Pillows would become prized as insulation. With winter approaching, wind whistled through the naked walls, and the gaps between the wooden floor slats were wide enough to let through an occasional mouse. Everyone wanted the bunks near the stove, so we drew lots.

Once a week we lined up for the gigantic shower room. This was such an assembly line that afterwards we just pulled on our skimpy clothes and went home damp and freezing. This made for many a cough and fever, so most of the time we kept clean with a bucket of warm water heated on the stove. The lack of privacy meant the children got a firm grounding in human anatomy, but each of us was so busy looking out for himself that before long nude bodies attracted little attention.

As soon as we had settled in, the children headed off to explore. From the front gate we could see a small chapel across the street, and next to it the "Stieglbauer Inn", a small restaurant that had catered to the construction and factory workers in years gone by. Across the barbed wire to the right of the camp was the "Böhler Works", a vast factory complex that had produced air defense weapons during the war. The real children's payoff seemed to be to the left and rear of the camp, each offering hills perfect for skiing. There would also be great sledding on the steep hillside to the left, with its ridge above; and out back we could use the logging trails.

The fun would have to wait, though. Since the only way out of the camp was through the heavily patrolled gate, and since we were behind a ten-foot fence, the hills and factory were really no playgrounds at all, just huge objects surrounding us on three sides. The adults had made clear we could leave only under very restricted circumstances. Short of an emergency trip to the hospital we would need a special, and rare, temporary written pass.

Rules are rules and kids are kids. Necessity helped us invent ways to come and go more or less at leisure. We could barely survive on our allotted rations; without a link to the outside world, our food would never improve and we would never have quite enough wood to fill the potbelly stove.

We could always obtain passes to go gather firewood. The woods were full of fallen branches, so there was always someone dragging wood back to their barracks. So long as we checked in before sunset, the Austrians' desire for free forest cleanup outweighed their distrust.

The woods turned out to be full of berries as well as branches. There were whole clearings full of raspberries, wild strawberries, and most surprisingly, dozens of mushroom species for us to bring back with our firewood.

Better nutrition also had its downside: we had to submit to several ritual doses of cod liver oil each week. Malnourished as we were, this was probably more important even than fresh produce; it may have saved our lives. So we hated it and would do anything to avoid it until they started following up with sugar cubes.

Freight trains came by the camp almost daily on their way to and from the factories, so the avant-garde kids decided to explore the railroad tracks next. A bonanza. While stoking the engine they often spilled precious chunks of coal. Come home with a bucket of coal and you were man of the hour.

Thinking up stories to get through the front gate soon became too much of a hassle. You couldn't go for firewood every day. So we took matters into our own hands and started cutting holes in the fence. The perimeter was quite long, so when they sealed one hole we could cut another.

Soon more and more refugees were leaving camp without authorization. We were easy to spot when we appeared in nearby villages; homeless people in rags do not exactly blend in. Worse, some of us were stealing fruit and more. Truth to tell, I was one of the fruit thieves, but fruit was all.

By the fall of 1945 the Austrians were up in arms about us: "gypsies", "damned refugees". They had disliked us from the start, and now they had a reason. We had turned into a band of scavengers, scrounging for food and clothing. No clothes were too hideous if they could help us prepare for the notorious six-month Austrian winter with its mountainous snowdrifts. As things stood, we had only the summer clothes we had arrived with from Lower Styria. If we still had shoes they were ankle-high boots with holes in the soles. Our woolen blankets would be our only excuse for overcoats.

We did barter honestly wherever possible. The more intrepid of us had discovered scrap iron, lead, copper and more while foraging through the many bombed-out factories in the neighborhood. Carrying the metals off was technically illegal, but they were after all abandoned, and guards cannot be everywhere at the same time, particularly when they are up against enterprising kids. The scrap dealer didn't care where the stuff came from. He drove a hard bargain but he was happy to pay in cash, enough for some used clothing.

This was the hour, just before my seventh birthday, when I first found my calling as a businessman. It seemed I had a knack for negotiation. My brother Richard was not so slick a pitchman, but when it came to heavy lifting he was Hercules by comparison. So we teamed up. He would be the "brawn" of the operation and I would be the "brains", or rather: the "mouth".

The hothouse of war and exile was forcing us and many like us to become the new men of Gottschee. Very few adult Gottscheer men were even left alive, and most of those were still in Russian captivity.

Christmas 1945 came and went completely unnoticed. No presents, no food, only the daily struggle for food and warmth. That winter was the worst we would ever experience, so cold that every venture outdoors became an expedition. The barracks walls were so leaky that icicles formed inside the room. Aside from the mess hall, and the bathhouse once a week, we hardly went out except to chop more wood for the stove. Worst was the call of nature in the middle of the night: the outhouse was some distance away through the frozen slush. It did a brisk 24-hour business, so the path was well-trodden. If you have any experience of Army latrines you will know the rest. If not, I will spare you the details. Suffice it to say that arctic temperatures do have the advantage of reducing stench.

Worse than the snow was maneuvering endlessly through the mud and puddles it left behind that spring. Hobo shoes meant constant wet feet, constant runny noses and coughs. The reward was a season of beautiful wild flowers, the rebirth of hope and optimism.

School began in earnest, with the children divided into classrooms by age. The Austrian teachers were so dedicated that I was happy to appear punctually each day of my first official school year, the year I learned to read and write and explore a new world.

They also built us a soccer field where children of all ages could play. Our team became strong enough to compete in Austrian school tournaments, though not before sustaining more than its share of injuries. Take it from me, barefoot soccer is a game unto itself. Along with the usual kicks in the shin you get your toes thoroughly tenderized. No shortage of bloodstains, but we loved every minute of it: we were alive and kicking, safe in Austria.

5

Tuning Up

One of the first classes in Camp #5. It is believed that the third boy from the left, on the top row is my brother.

Tuning Up

By the middle of 1946 it was clear there would be no fast track into the outside economy. We would have to work ourselves out of this poverty and captivity using every ounce of blood, sweat and cunning we could muster.

Not that any doubt remained about our ability to survive. Mama was a constant exemplar of faith and determination. Yes, we were living in barracks. Yes, we were poor. But things were looking up. Her incredible optimism never wavered. On the surface we had precious little to sing about, yet sing we did, with Mama as lead soprano. The glorious memory of those sessions fills me with respect for her cleverness in distracting and energizing us.

Mama announced she had met a farmer up in the mountains who had made her an attractive job offer, helping with the harvest. Not only would her wages be paid daily in food, but also she was allowed to bring her children along.

Armed with her day pass, we left the main gate behind and hiked up the mountain, passing through villages nestled higher and higher in the woods and on the hillsides. Mama could not stop pointing out the spectacular views of the valley below. She burst into song and we were soon yodeling for joy at the top of our lungs. The Austrians who saw us go by must have thought this remarkable coming from "gypsy beggars"—what on earth did the likes of us have to sing about?

At long last the road leveled off in a large meadow and we saw the farmhouse and outbuildings at the crest of the next hill. There were animals grazing and feeding in every direction: horses, cows, sheep, lambs, pigs, all sorts of chickens and roosters. The farm was bustling with people picking potatoes, cutting and processing wheat, husking corn in a shed. Clearly the owner was not lacking for crops. What he needed was help, and Mama was ready.

We reported to him and he explained she would be back in late afternoon, at the end of the workday. Until then we were on our own, unless we wanted to help the cherry crew. The trees were bursting with fruit, and if we helped pick we could eat as many as our heart desired.

Who could pass on a deal like that? As we worked we kept literally stuffing our mouths with the luscious cherries. We even made earrings of them. The pits we spat out like machine gunners. It was heaven on earth.

Purgatory followed in due course as our stomachs submitted their bill: first bloating, then intense nausea interspersed with mad dashes to the outhouse. When we rejoined Mama we were exhausted and rather sore, yet still ecstatic. She told us we had learned a valuable lesson: never let overindulgence ruin a good thing.

Mama was happy too: the farmer had given her almost 45 pounds of potatoes and ten fresh eggs for her labor. He was quite satisfied with her work. She was invited back many times and returned with a whole range of staples we had nearly forgotten: bread, milk, smoked ham, even two chickens. Camp food never looked the same again. Life was good.

Until the day when Mama suddenly fell ill, so ill that the infirmary nurse could not help her. They rushed her to the city hospital at Bruck an der Mur, leaving Richard and me to face our roommates alone.

We quickly found out that relatives are not always your truest friends in times of dire need. Even with relatives living right in our room, little help was forthcoming. Of course, my aunt had her own problems. Her husband too was gone and she had five mouths to feed. But such reflections could not replenish our dwindling reserves. For that we would have to start working the firewood circuit again.

Returning to the woods, we became increasingly expert at spotting and gathering the non-poisonous mushrooms and berries. We had buckets full, for both business and pleasure. Mushrooms can be served many great ways, from soup to sauteed, but they are even better when you can toss them in with a few bartered eggs. Berries made great jam and marmalade to drown the strange taste of the white camp bread, but we could also trade them for milk, or a slice of ham or chicken.

It hurt nonetheless when people started treating us as orphans. Was Mama really never coming home again? Was there no more hope of escaping from this god-forsaken refugee camp?

In fact they returned her to us one day looking not the least bit the worse for wear. The mystery of her illness was never really solved; all she would ever say was "I was very sick, but I'm as good as new again." The happy days of singing and extra food returned, but Mama remained a touch bitter toward her unhelpful sister. Mama had viewed us all as one big family and had always contributed generously to what she thought was the common cause. Now she saw she had been a little too trusting.

We no longer accompanied Mama up the mountain; school was in session and we had chores of our own. If we left, who would bring in the wood and coal? And there was even more important kid business to consider, such as soccer games.

Virtue is sometimes a mistake, and perhaps if we had played hooky with Mama we would have missed out on the mumps outbreak late that spring. We did seem to recover completely, so we were bewildered when not long thereafter a whole group of us kids was bussed off to a children's camp for "recuperation".

This episode was to remain as unfathomable as my mother's illness. Was it quarantine? My room held about ten children in two rows of neat little cribs. Nurses came in regularly with pills, shots, and brusque orders that we keep quiet and go to sleep. The harsh disorientation kept sending some of the kids on crying marathons, and one nurse was so mean that she shook them until they shut up.

When the dreams came this time, they were Mama coming to pick me up, and I awoke to crushing disappointment in the dark midnight ward. By the time she appeared for a visit I had lost count of the days. She was not allowed to take me when she left. No matter how tough a survivor I had become, I was still just seven and there was no escaping the traumatic impression that we would never meet again. I felt completely abandoned and even imagined she no longer thought me worth the trouble of keeping.

Then without fanfare I too rematerialized in Camp 5, "good as new again". Who knows what dreadful fate their skill had spared me.

6

I'm a Believer

Holy Confirmation 1947—Cousin Erwin, Edwin, Mama, Richie and Papa

I'm a Believer

The summer of 1946 began undramatically enough. There was no end in sight, but our mother had reason to be happy with her newfound success as breadwinner. The farmers admired her work ethic and kept asking her to return, while others rotted in camp waiting for handouts. We could not build capital, but we ate better than most.

Richard and I did our part, vowing to picking as many berries as possible before the first frost, and scouring the countryside for scrap. Iron was a drug on the market, but copper and lead were in short supply, guaranteeing a tidy return.

Meanwhile the initial trickle of care packages from America had become a steady stream. Some of them contained not only food staples but clothing, even the shoes we needed so badly.

School was the brightest promise for the refugee children, and in our family good grades were mandatory. Mama reasoned an education would at least gain her children a place in the Austrian mainstream. Here Richard was at an advantage. He was naturally smarter than I and labored diligently toward his dream of becoming an engineer through the refugee apprenticeship program at the Böhler Works. Richard won many of the autographed books and other trophies the teachers awarded as prizes. I still wanted to be a butcher like my cousin Karl. The few prizes I won cost me much greater effort, like my occasional high grades. My advantage was the guts and determination that have served me all my life.

Thanks to the love of singing Mama had instilled in us, we needed no encouragement to join the children's choir, which became surprisingly accomplished and was frequently invited to appear at orphanages and senior centers. The smiling, appreciative audiences boosted our pride and won us some recognition from Austrians who had seen us as "gypsy" zeros.

Summer break in August gave us weeks to play soccer and run through the woods. One afternoon during an intramural soccer match my cousin, who was even younger than I, came scampering across to the field and began jumping up and down, shouting "Edwin, Edwin, your father has come home!" The silly cruelty of the joke stunned me and I actually slapped her, but she was too excited really to notice. She kept repeating the news, swearing it was true—"Just go to your barracks, he's there"—and finally I just had to check it out. I ran through the camp so recklessly that I stumbled and fell several times before I arrived in the midst of a celebration.

People were jumping up and down with delight at the sight of a man so skeletal that he might have been a concentration camp survivor, even a zombie. The impossible had indeed come to pass: moving closer up, one could see in him the healthy, robust man we remembered. It was true, and the truth was a miracle, a resurrection. Papa had come home from the war. He was alive. Barely, but alive.

Papa held up a large jar of real honey and a loaf of black bread. He had carried them with him for days, hoping for this unforgettable moment. We spread the honey thick and rich and the story of his odyssey began to unfold.

When last we saw him he had been in training after his induction into the Wehrmacht. Being a horse specialist, he was assigned to the field artillery at the Russian front, bringing heavy equipment to the front lines.

There had been countless close calls. When a shell hit his horses directly, killing a whole team of six, he had just dismounted to water them from a freezing pond nearby; the explosion hurled him into the water, where he was forced to remain all night as advancing Russian troops swarmed past him. When he found his way back to his unit the next day he was a living icicle, his uniform frostbitten into his skin. He endured three days of delirium until the fever broke. Even this was more time than the desperate situation allowed, and a day or so later he was back on active duty.

Despite the many more battles he was drawn into before the end came the next May, he spent the rest of his life grateful to God for having him sent to the Russian rather than the American front. Among the scores of US-born second-generation Gottscheers who fought and died on the American side were two of my paternal cousins. One volunteered for the Navy, the other for the Army Airborne, where he was killed parachuting into Normandy. He is buried among the thousands of American soldiers who died in that fierce battle, the turning point of the war. My father would not have been able to live with himself had he fired the shot that killed his own nephew.

My favorite incident was a missed bet just before my father's capture near Stalingrad. Word had come that the war was over and the soldiers should escape however they could. My father and three other Wehrmacht soldiers had ditched their rifles but were still in uniform. Wandering through the countryside, they stumbled upon an abandoned farmhouse. Inside they found a carton of cans that looked like food. They opened one to find escargots, a delicacy less coveted on the battlefield than in French restaurants. "Can you imagine, they had snails in those cans."

They did also find a case of wine bottles, and these they knew what to do with. Naturally, since they had not eaten for days, it took little wine to get them blind drunk. My father's comrades staggered off, each in his own daze. One was going "home", another in search of food, the third into the woods "to kill myself". This was no way to say a final goodbye, but my father was far too relaxed to object; he had his own agenda, something to do with veering toward a nearby tree.

He was awakened by something hard jammed up against his nose. His eyes opened into the muzzle of a rifle with a very nervous young Russian soldier at the other end, motioning him to stand and walk in front. Papa, none too eager to be shot by a panicky kid, was delighted to oblige. He was marched off to a Russian Army encampment where he encountered hundreds of other German soldiers who had suffered the same fate. With the characteristically Russian mixture of discipline and loud cursing, they received their diplomas as POWs.

Growing up under the Yugoslavian yoke, my father had plenty of "street smarts". He had long since discarded his ID, realizing his fluent Slavic languages might soon earn him considerably more affection than native German. When the Russians demanded his name, rank and serial number, the name was Slavic. He uttered not one German word as he recounted the sad tale he had rehearsed: an innocent lad railroaded into the Wehrmacht from his home in Slovenia. Papa was certain this ruse saved his life. Not bad for a guy with little formal education.

Personal effects had to be surrendered before interrogation. Some of the Germans still had their wedding rings; there were even watches, which led to some comedy. The Russians fell to quarreling over their booty, which contained far more wristwatches than pocketwatches. One of them, curiously upset because he had received the rarer of the two sorts, discovered that one of the prisoners was a watchmaker. He walked up to him and shoved a gun in his face, ordering him to "make two out of this one"—two wristwatches. When the German shook his head, the Russian shook with anger, until his comrade clued him in.

Once the preliminaries were out of the way, the prisoners were lined up for a forced march to parts unknown. After a full day's grueling march they arrived at a railroad station, where they were ordered into tightly packed cattle trains and were soon underway. No one told them where they were headed, but it was north, colder and colder, with only one piece of bread and cup of water a day. Only the heat of their huddled bodies kept them from freezing to death. It was days before the train stopped at a deserted station. Other than barracks near the mountains, there was nothing in sight but vast expanses of ice. No one had to be told this was Siberia, the land of coal mines and slave labor.

The Russians wasted no time breaking the prisoners down into work groups. Before they were forced into the mines there was a lecture on prison camp rules and regulations. This was delivered first in Russian, and my father discovered he could understand some of it through family resemblances to the Slavic languages. A useful addition to his arsenal. Next came the German version, which my father pretended not to understand. The whole thing blared through the ubiquitous camp loudspeakers which were to become a constant background.

The daily rations were a piece of bread and something that passed for soup, sometimes with cabbage, almost never with meat. Plus a curious nutritional supplement: Russian cigarettes.

After a brief runthrough of the day's quotas the prisoners descended into the dark mines via a gigantic dumbwaiter, which also hauled up filled baskets of coal, "dogs". If you missed your quota you forfeited your daily bread, and in some cases your life. It is hard to believe, but my father said some prisoners were so addicted to smoking that they were willing to give up their bread for extra cigarettes. He was happy to trade his cigarettes for enhanced survival. Without the bread the watery 'soup' would swell you up like a balloon.

Every day a few prisoners were carried out dead for sheer lack of energy to survive. Many others died in the frequent explosions, fires and cave-ins.

The accommodations were horrible: freezing barracks with hardly any blankets. Papa swore it was so cold that your breath froze on your face. If you had to go relieve yourself outside it literally froze before it hit the ground.

Early on, my father befriended the Russian civilian girl who collected the tags and tallied the production. The prisoners hung one tag on every full dog they sent up, and she monitored the quotas for each team. Papa quickly mastered enough Russian to learn she could be executed for even chatting with the prisoners. A few conversations convinced him of her courage and cured him of any prejudices towards Russians. If they sometimes seemed nasty it was because their only news of the outside world was the government propaganda that blared over the loudspeakers. Given the pressure of their brutal orders, they could scarcely resist being indoctrinated, but beneath this the civilians at least were utterly decent.

Papa knew all the men would eventually die in the mines if they had to maintain their heavy quotas indefinitely on nothing but bread and water. It struck him that you could inflate your production figures if you could attach more than one tag to each dog. He managed to persuade the girl to turn a blind eye when he attached extra tags. She even went him one further and threw extra tags into Papa's team bucket herself. They cooked the books for a long time and Papa praised her compassion for the rest of his life.

Partial escape from the quotas bought him some time and kept alive the tiny hope of eventual freedom. Escape was out of the question, since even if you got away there was nowhere to go but icy death. But as you will have noticed by now, our family was driven by a phenomenal determination to survive. This trait was a lifesaver and my father's perseverance shows we inherited it.

Rumors began to circulate about negotiations with the German and Yugoslavian governments, on repatriating POWs. Supposedly the Russians were progressing faster with the Yugoslavians than with the Germans. This made sense: Germany had lost the war, while Tito's Yugoslavia was now an ally. If Papa could maintain his Slovenian cover he might well end up in the first wave of releases. This gave him even more incentive to stay alive.

It would not be a cakewalk; the Russians were well aware there might be fraud. Every prisoner was interviewed by many different people, but they interviewed supposedly Yugoslavian prisoners most often of all, using language experts and repeating questions ad nauseam to trip up Germans in disguise. My father felt sure he had passed their test.

Rumor became formal announcement that a release was imminent, and when the list of names appeared a few weeks later, my father was delighted to find his Slavic alias on it. He was inches from freedom, though being on the list was not quite a guarantee: several men died tragically during the preparations for transport.

The cattle trains must have been a little easier to bear when you knew they were heading clear across the Russian border. The journey wound through Czechoslovakia, then a tense leg through occupied Hungary, Austria and finally Yugoslavia. Every day there was a rest stop for prisoners to eat and relieve themselves.

On the third day, one of the Serb prisoners confronted my father in front of a whole group of Slovenians, accusing him of being German. This was a bolt from the blue. Papa denied it and went on the attack, calling the Serb a liar. The rest of the prisoners joined in and thrashed the Serb until he agreed to retract his accusations.

The Slovenians knew the truth. They told my father not to show his face at any of the remaining stops; they would bring him his food and water. Whenever an inspection came they all bunched up at the front to hide him. The Serb was in such fear for his life that he kept his suspicions entirely to himself.

Ironically, Papa passed only miles from our camp on his way through the British sector in Styria. He had no idea whether we had made it to Austria, but he was determined to reach Kerschdorf and the farm, to begin his search for us, praying we were still alive.

They released him in Marburg, just a few miles short of the southern Austrian border. From there he made his way on foot to Königsberg and Kerschdorf.

Here the real marvel occurred. As he walked up the hill he could see right away that the farm was back in high gear A Slovenian couple stood in front of the house, watching Papa come up the hill. When his face came into focus they started running towards him. It was the original owners. They hugged and kissed him and told him that when they had been liberated at the end of the war they had returned to find their farm vacated just as he had promised. His kindness had made all the difference for them.

They could not help him find us, only fill him in on the killings of Gottscheers and the burnings of Gottscheer farms. They admitted their sons had escaped and joined the partisans when the Germans invaded. Their sons had arranged for us to be spared during the bloodbath. What goes around, comes around.

Papa was their honorary relative. They fed and clothed him and gave him a bed. But even if he had not been eager to move on, Kerschdorf was by no means safe for a returning German soldier. The sons provided him safe passage on the first leg of his quest, but they had to be so circumspect that it was weeks before he discovered even that there had been Gottscheer wagon trains from the Ranner Triangle to Austria.

The sons brought him on horseback to a remote spot on the Austrian border. After they escorted him across on foot, they thanked him one last time and took their leave, wishing him luck.

Papa trudged along, cold and hungry, until he discovered there were refugee camps in Klagenfurt. This was in Carinthia, whence our ancestors had come in 1330, so he thought they might have put us there. He was almost right; there were in fact many Gottscheers in the Pfeffernitz camp, just not us. But he was able to get a list of other camps with Gottscheer refugees, and he visited them one by one until he hit pay dirt in Kapfenberg at Camp #5. A shiver must have gone up his spine when the administration told him they had two families with the name Stalzer.

One pilgrimage had ended. Another was about to begin.

7

The Big Thaw

My father's cooper's bench

The Big Thaw

Morale was high as school began that fall. The family had weathered severe trials and tribulations, and with our father back we were confident the worst was over. Meaning had returned to the word 'future', renewing our vigor and determination to make something of ourselves. Refugee camps were merely a detour on the road to success.

My father had wasted no time seeking gainful employment, registering for any job the camp administration and the Böhler Works could offer. Soon he was bringing home cash from carpentry and repair work at the factory. Basics like clothing and utensils were no longer out of reach.

Our exile from the official economy was over, and not a moment too soon; we were sick of using discarded milk and coffee cans for pots and pans. No more settling for mere survival. We had a whole new outlook, the fresh optimism we needed to fight our way clear of the camp and the handouts.

Part of the barracks metamorphosed into a master cooper's workshop. Papa was convinced the local farmers needed beautiful wooden containers: bathtubs, butter churns, buckets, you name it. He talked the village smith into fronting him custom draw knives in exchange for a share in the profits. Logs also materialized in front of the barracks; they were meticulously split into boards of various lengths and stacked in a ring to dry just in time for the onset of winter.

Production of samples began even before the snows came. Papa had devised an ingenious foot-controlled vise running up through the top of the workbench; its hinged jaw let him quickly fix a board at each new angle, freeing his hands to concentrate on the fine details. He took his bench outside and I watched him for days on end, drawing his knives toward him across the boards, trimming and fashioning each piece to round it off.

In our digital era we forget the extreme skill required to make a wooden bucket or butter churn by hand. The refugees gathered in crowds to marvel at my father's dexterity. Each piece had to be shaved and planed to perfection or it would not fit into the jigsaw puzzle. Paradoxically, it was water that made each vessel watertight: by filling it up, Papa expanded the wood until not a drop could leak through. Each barrel, each churn, each bucket was a masterpiece of folk art; to this day I have seen nothing anywhere to rival their complete smoothness.

Now that we had samples, it was showtime for our marketing division: Richard, now all of ten years old, and myself at a good seven and "almost six months". The very first demonstrations of the smaller items made it obvious the nearby farmers had never seen such quality. It was no secret that we were refugees, but plainly these were more than just buckets, and just as plainly we were more than just beggars or scam artists. We had something special to offer and we carried ourselves with corresponding dignity. Startled by the superiority of our merchandise, and intrigued by the patter of a rather cute blue-eyed blond motormouth, they were eager to negotiate.

We first discussed their needs in detail, then settled on a price and delivery date. The price varied with the size and intricacy of the vessel. A small bucket might command only eggs, milk and potatoes, while a large bathtub or fancy wine barrel might be good for a whole smoked ham. The best margin was on our flagship item, the double-decker butter churn. Atop its barrel-like outer shell was the slot for the smaller bucket, which in turn had a cover insert with a center hole. You took out the cover, pushed the plunger handle through it from below, replaced the cover assembly and churned away. This came in three sizes and everybody wanted one.

Negotiation turned me into a formidable salesman, returning to camp in triumph with sheaves of signed orders. The whole barracks congratulated us and we soon had them all on the payroll. Some procured the lumber, by fair means or foul. Others cut logs to Papa's specifications, or split and stacked them. The kids foraged for metal strips strong enough to hoop barrels. Everyone on the assembly line got their share of the take.

Richard and I wanted to do more than just sales, so we decided to split logs. He would hold and I would split. Like all fatal ideas, this seemed to work fine. Richard held each log upright, nimbly stepping aside just before the axe fell. Until I brought it down full force on his finger. The gush of blood, my brother's primal scream and his terrified wailing meant my ignominious return to our traditional kneeling punishment, for the first time since Lower Styria. Wow, things were really back to normal. Thank God it wasn't his arm.

Banished from the tool rack, I learned to supplement my sales role with bookkeeping. For a kid less than eight years old I was quite sharp. Every customer got a page in my notebook, covering all their contracts, due dates, outstanding balances: 5 hams, 10 kilos of bacon, 100 kilos of potatoes, 5 chickens, 20 liters of milk. We did did not always have the manpower to drag home full payment on delivery, nor the refrigeration to store it indefinitely, so we did rounds collecting installments: a ham here, a gallon of milk there. Since this could not be done simply on a handshake and a memory, it fell to me to keep tabs and get signatures on every payment. The positive feedback from my system was so indelible that years later it still motivated me to become certified as an accountant.

With me as sales manager and bookkeeper, the hard physical work fell to Richard, who was better equipped to haul the merchandise up and the bounty down. It was an ideal business for two kids. Great merchandise and a good production line made selling easy. Price negotiations were trickier, but we soon learned what the market would bear.

The family also picked berries throughout the fall. The sunny hillsides northwest of town were full of large clearings where the trees had been harvested and not replanted. Here we discovered raspberries and blueberries by the ton. This excited Papa's business instincts. The Austrians would pay top dollar for perfect dessert and pie berries; even squashed jam and juice berries fetched some money.

Papa had made a beautiful flat berry barrel with leather straps that let you carry it like a backpack. We Stalzers were an industrious bunch and we filled it up on every trip, six or eight cubic feet, along with the half-gallon buckets we had made from discarded food and coffee cans. You punched holes for wire handles, and presto, a bucket you could hang on your belt while working your way into the deep bushes, fighting off the wasps and snakes, not altogether unlike the ancestors forging the first path to Gottschee.

The others noticed we had hit pay dirt and tried to shadow us. To keep them from stealing our claim we sometimes had to leave camp as early as two in the morning. We made it a family outing and always managed to turn work into play, competing with one another and calling out each can we emptied into the berry bucket. Mush was taboo, only perfectly ripe berries would do.

Come noon the whistle blew and we clamored for our daily picnic. Mama always packed a great lunch, things that would not spoil in the heat: smoked ham, sausages, bread with smoked bacon. We filled our cups with mountain spring water and dropped in fizzy disks just like flavored Alka-Selzer: raspberry, cherry, sometimes even strawberry.

Not all memories of the woods are so idyllic. Very early one morning we stumbled across a man in a deer blind and realized we had been routinely trespassing on the turf of the Jägermeister, the master ranger. We were disrupting the game preserve of the only person

Austrian towns honor with a hunting license, the man who supplies the butcher shops with game. He did not take our intrusion calmly; in fact, he threatened to kill us, backing it up with live fire. These must have been warning shots into the air, but they seemed aimed at us and we fled for our lives.

The local hornets did not like trespassers any better. I once stumbled into a nest the size of a basketball, triggering a monstrous swarm that sent us tearing and tumbling in terror down the hillside into the cold stream. Stalzer luck let us walk away with only drenched clothes and a few bruises, routine business expenses.

Even the woods themselves once demanded tribute: an entire day's labor. Papa was gingerly making his way back down the steep hillside at day's end, the harvest strapped to his shoulder, when he lost his balance and went bouncing all the way to the road. We scooped up many of the berries strewn in every direction, but they were badly crushed and would have to join our private stock as raspberry juice. Laughter was in order, since Papa had escaped unharmed; also our loudest singing, all the way to the main road, to cap off the adventure.

Our second Christmas in camp saw the barracks well stocked with durable winter rations and our accounts receivable well stocked with perishables. Smoked meats in our larder, dairy and produce close by, plenty of seasoned coopering wood stacked out front. My father had been able to set up production indoors by the stove, partly because people had helpfully moved their bunks to make room, and partly for the sadder reason that some of our elderly roommates had died, with no new refugees to replace them.

To celebrate the return of real Christmas, we kids earmarked a live spruce right after St. Nicholas' Day—the sixth of December—and returned to take it later in the month. I do mean 'take'; the tree was admittedly as illegal as it was beautiful. It became a yearly tradition to find the perfect tree, drag it back through the snow until we were frozen stiff as icicles, then soak our feet in a hot bath while drinking piping hot tea.

Everyone found or made something to hang on the tree, mainly the traditional edible decorations we had loved in Lower Styria. Throughout the camp and in the villages beyond you could smell the butter cookies mothers were baking. There were foil-wrapped walnuts impaled on toothpicks and hung by colorful strings; construction-paper angels and stars with cotton border strips and sparkling glitter; apples, pears, oranges, occasional candy; and real candles everywhere.

Richard and I were startled when our father unveiled our presents from the Christchild: a sled and two pairs of skis, all handmade. By comparison with the store-bought skis of the Austrian kids, ours were makeshift, with bindings made out of bedsprings, vaguely curled using water vapor. The most sophisticated thing on the sled was the metal strips on the bottom of the curved wooden runners. But they all had the charm of the antique skis we would see in museums years later. Bottom line: we had skis. We had a sled. We had to try them out right away.

Before Christmas Day was over we had sidestepped up the hill and zoomed down, but the friction was a little disappointing. Then someone clued us in: you have to wax skis. After we dripped hot wax from a candle and melted it in with an iron, we were greased lightning. We were also an accident waiting to happen: no skills, marginal equipment, just rocketing along until something knocked us into a somersault. Yet no harm ever came to us either on the ski slope or blasting down the logging track on the sled.

My father's spectacular return, and our victory over poverty, made for an exquisite contrast with the previous year, a radiance later Christmases would never quite match. Gottscheer tradition was reborn, our parents spreading their wealth of food so broadly that no one bothered to pick up their mess hall rations that day. A rich man would not have thought twice about the hard cider that washed down the smoked delicacies and cheeses, but to us it offered the thrill of a quantum improvement. For one glorious day we forgot our problems, aglow with good resolutions.

Outside, snow had blanketed the camp six feet deep. Our clothing and shoes were not really adequate to the momentous task of clearing pathways, but it was still a child's winter wonderland. Once we made it to the hills there was sledding, sleigh riding and skiing every day after school, plus the snow games kids have invented since the world began. These were some of the brightest moments in our otherwise bleak routine. When the sun cracked the thick four-foot icicles off the barracks, they became swords for mock battles. We built walls, castles, igloos, all the fortifications you need for professional snowball fights. On sunny days they would start to melt, but by the next morning there would be a thick new coat of glistening ice.

The price we paid for our ice capades was to spend months wading philosophically through freezing ankle-deep water and mud. Clearing the drifts had meant shoveling up snow mountains so high that they kept melting well into April, turning the unpaved paths into miniature streams and lakes. Ideal conditions for colds and flu, but this too would pass.

Nature takes its course for rich and poor alike, but being poor we were better able than the prosperous villagers to savor the colorful beauty of the spring countryside, the woods and meadows jumping back to life, laughing with thousands of wildflowers and blossoms, green grass, fresh mushroom pickings popping up everywhere. Our gloom gave way to joyful song and games, resolute study and work.

Being a true family again, watching our father work to support us, increased our hope of one day venturing out into the Austrian mainstream. Most refugees had much sadder luck. Many of their fathers, brothers and cousins would not return from Russia until the early fifties, if they returned from war at all. And though the Austrians did not much like us, at least we had Austrian ancestors; non-German-speakers were outright pariahs.

We also had the ultimate advantage: the unswerving Catholic devotion that had brought the land of Gottschee through disaster after disaster. Our little converted barracks church was a hub of activity, and not just on the Sabbath. Custom and tradition were once again filling our lives with baptisms, first communions, confirmations, weddings, funerals and religious holidays.

After Christmas the most important season was Easter, with its gigantic procession. The first hint was Ash Wednesday, the beginning of Lent, when we all went to morning mass and the parish priest traced the sign of the cross in ash on our foreheads. This signified forty days of fasting, until Easter week began with the consecration of pussy willow branches on Palm Sunday. Yes, pussy willows.

All through Easter week, sometimes as early as Lent, the children had been preparing for the Easter Saturday "fire festival". They combed the woods for something that would stay lit for an entire morning: an ideally rotten tree stump, with just a little solidity left, or perhaps a choice fungus. These were dried to perfection, and when the priest lit the holy fire in front of the church early Saturday morning, all the kids rushed to light the tip of their wands. If the wood flared up, you knew you had a dud. The best just glowed red, with no flame.

People were expecting us as we rushed from barracks to barracks and house to house, and they let us in to open their woodstoves and light their kindling with a deft stroke of our holy embers: a special blessing from the church, a house call to ward off illness. They gave us some coins and we were merrily on our way to the next stop, hoping our research had paid off with a wand that would keep us in the race all the way to the finish.

On Easter Sunday the priest and deacons led a flock of many hundreds to High Mass, where they blessed whatever food our mothers had managed to fit into their baskets. Upon our return home the consecrated food became our Sunday feast.

Easter was also prime time for Confirmation and First Communion. Our parents decided that I would first take communion on the day of Richard's confirmation, with our cousin Erwin traveling from the Leibniz camp to be our sponsor. Then it occurred to them that I might as well be confirmed the very same day.

The sacred event took place at the tiny chapel across the street from the main camp entrance. It called for our first photographs since arriving in camp: the entire family including Erwin. They are classic World War Two refugee shots. Both parents are emaciated enough to pass for death camp survivors, particularly my father, with Siberia just six months behind him. My father and cousin are both wearing surprisingly dapper suits, my mother her best print dress. Richard and I are in brand new khaki shorts and shirts, right out of the box, a present from our aunt in New York. Hardly a confirmation suit, but we are happy and proud nonetheless.

Weddings made kids happy for some of the same reasons as the fire festival. Tradition ordained another long procession to the church, with the whole community dressed to the nines and the bridal party throwing coins to the children lined up at the side of the road. They also threw candy, which was still very rare. We loved diving for these treats and all the adults loved to watch us go at it.

The only sour note came when my maternal aunt Olga married a boy from what was once the village next door, back in Yugoslavia. At the reception I somehow ticked off the groom's cousin and he threatened to smack me around. Chances are he had his reasons, but whatever they were, I never did warm up to this "uncle" and avoided him at all costs even much later on in America.

America. It was popping up more and more in our conversation. Before our father returned, emigrating there had seemed about as likely as a trip to the moon. Now it was becoming a serious goal. Papa wanted to ensure his children would never again face the cruel whims of war. He feared the Russians swooping south to kidnap boys for their coal mines. America was the only place where hard work meant a real chance of success. Not that his own future mattered: surely, at the ripe old age of 36, he had already entered his latter days. The point was a better life for the kids.

None of us yet realized what patience was required for the long road of applications and interviews emigrants had to travel before they could sail the Atlantic; but once we started tuning in to refugee resettlement programs, the USA kept coming out on top, with its wonderful support system of Gottscheer clubs and organizations.

Synchronicity had gone into action. The director told the children's choir it was to perform for "a very important American" who was coming to see firsthand how Gottscheers were doing in the camps. None of us spoke a word of English, but by the time we gathered on the soccer field to serenade the American delegation we had learned "God Bless America" phonetically.

The "very important American" was Adolf Schauer, the Gottscheer-American attorney spearheading the Gottscheer Hilfswerk, the key relief and immigration organization in New York. Performing for him was a great honor and he expressed his enjoyment with a speech that would set the tone for years to come. Though our Homeland was surely lost, he assured us hope lived on. Gottscheer Americans were united in their vow to reunite their countrymen, to exchange the burden of refugee homelessness for the dignity of citizenship.

8

Busting Out

My favorite Karl May book entitled "WINNETOU"

Busting Out

An amazing number of doors opened to us once Papa was back in the driver's seat. With the Austrian economy recovering, the British tired of occupation and the Austrian government took over the camps. Austrians had the jobs they needed and could consider hiring refugees. A third-generation Gottscheer farmer like my father was a natural for the local farm economy, since he could do everything from agriculture to animal husbandry in his sleep.

Papa was hell-bent on getting ahead, and his constant probing revealed that if he could land a civilian job over and above his coopering, our family could demonstrate the self-sufficiency required for a transfer to Camp 7 in Marein.

Camp 7 was the next best thing to freedom. Normally refugees could leave it only for jobs, schools, and essential errands. But there were no physical restrictions, no barbed wire or locked gates, just a symbolic fence. Each side of each barracks was divided into individual rooms. Instead of coexisting with 25 people in a room, a family could have two rooms to itself, plus a plot in the vegetable garden just outside. Schooling was mandatory for children, and since there was no camp school, we would be promoted into the Austrian school system.

If anyone was qualified for this deal it was Papa, and he pulled out all the stops. First he landed an ideal job in a large Marein vineyard, supervising the gathering and pressing of the grapes during the harvest and working hay, livestock and the rest in the off season.

This job had some great perks for kids. You have not tasted grape juice until you have had it straight from the presses, sweet as honey in the few days before it starts fermenting. And when the wagons pulled up to unload their grapes at the railroad station across the street, we needed only show up at the fence to gather whole bunches.

The authorities shared our satisfaction with Papa's credentials, and when we were among the names announced for relocation we saw a unique blend of envy and admiration on the faces of our fellow refugees.

Richard and I were duly registered at the Marein Public School in September 1947, and after a few days settling into our two private rooms, our parents dropped us off for our first day as Austrian schoolchildren. Actually, though we fit in physically, our home haircuts and clean but unfashionable clothes instantly gave us away as foreigners and refugees. To the Austrian children we looked like suspicious gypsies. What threw them was that we spoke German.

After a few weeks Richard stopped coming to school with me. At eleven he was old enough for the commute to the junior high in Kapfenberg, where English was a required course. He was on his way to high school and an engineering degree. Along with this academic milestone came a new sled and store-bought skis, the cheapest in the store, but no longer homemade. The road past the camp from Lorenzen ran downhill into Marein, so weather permitting we often went to school on our skis or by sled. A delightful way to make an entrance, but we paid for it on the way home, hauling our wooden steeds back up the hill.

The Austrian children were so standoffish at first that I was not sure trying to make friends would be worthwhile. They started to warm up to me by the end of the first year, when they realized that "the refugee" was not just moving up the class charts but had become a star student. Determined to remain near the top of the class, I worked much harder than they did and the teacher often pointed me out as an example of what hard work can accomplish. The boost to my self-esteem spurred my resolve, and little by little they began consulting me on math and geography. The flip side was learning to ignore the jealousy more conformist kids feel when inspiration and perspiration lead to recognition.

Franz Schichtler was the only boy in my class not ashamed to be my friend from the start. We hung out after school and he took a lively interest in my saga, impressed with our endurance and faith. He told his parents about me and they encouraged him to invite me home for study sessions. This was a tremendous treat. Franz lived just five minutes from school at an address I never forgot, 9 Main Street. By my standards his modest home was a mansion: brick and stone, with three full bedrooms, a living room and kitchen, and the twin wonders of indoor plumbing and electricity. The best we had ever had was a naked bulb dangling from a wire, but here there were gorgeous lamps, milk and cookies every afternoon. I was not a statistic but a real person.

A little too real at times: Franz's parents were intellectuals and my streetwise example threw a wrench or two into their educational agenda. During the long summer break of 1948 I initiated their carefully sheltered son into the mysteries of killing and dressing rabbits and chickens, making and using weapons, even crossbows. We had all kinds of adventures, climbing trees in the woods, falling into the river, doing ethnomethodological research in an authentic refugee camp. Huckleberry Finn had nothing on us.

If Franz's parents had not exactly planned on raising a tough guy, Franz himself certainly enjoyed acquiring street credibility. Once our daily chores were done there was always some fresh mission, too highly classified for the untutored ears of our parents. There were many bombed-out factories in urgent need of exploration, metals eagerly awaiting their trip to the junk dealer: business for me, kicks for my affluent friend. We even infiltrated a burned-out bunker. Its entrance, half submerged in water up to our waists, had been completely sealed off with concrete slabs, but once we removed them the place looked inviting and we headed in sideways, feeling our way until we could squeeze no further. Suddenly we realized we were wedged in a pitch-black tunnel, never to be heard from again. Zest for adventure turned into fear and hasty retreat.

The bunker was just one artificial curiosity among the countless natural caves begging for exploration up in the hills. Armed with ropes and the hands-free flashlights you clip to your shirt, Franz and I enlisted two other boys from camp to take on the most inviting cave. Its entrance was on a ledge fifteen feet above the path. About sixty feet in, it split in two and we chose the larger right fork. The air grew bitter cold as we penetrated deep into the mountain, ending up in a spacious cavern. When we sat down and shone our lights around we spooked dozens of bats. Their frantic careening scared us witless. Worse, one of our flashlights began flickering. It was time to clear out, but the way back proved trickier than the way in: we came to a difficult fork we had not even noticed. What saved us was the foresight of one boy the rest of us had mocked as he tied his rope to a tree outside the cave. That rope guided us out as surely as Hänsel's bread crumbs in the fairy tale, and the last laugh was on us.

Franz traded me something wonderful for my delinquency lessons: access to his extensive library, including a complete set of Karl May's adventure books. We spent many an hour lying back and holding these volumes in the air as they whisked us on make-believe journeys to the farthest corners of the earth, to *The Kingdom of the Silver Lion* or *The Treasure Island*, via *Unknown Paths*, in the company of the *Oil Prince* or the *Half Blood*, or on the *Slave Caravan*.

My favorite by far was *Winnetou*, published in three volumes between 1876 and 1893. It chronicles the friendship between a noble Red Indian chief—the Apache Winnetou—and his blood brother Old Shatterhand, an American pioneer of German descent. Winnetou is the only Native American with the power to unite the quarreling Southwestern tribes threatened by construction of the first transcontinental railroad. His murder at the hands of gold-grubbing thugs forecloses the possibility of an equitable settlement with the whites, foreshadowing the death of his people.

May's first-person narration draws the reader into the action through the eyes of Old Shatterhand. You almost feel you are the character. At times I would just close my eyes and lie there dreaming of the beautiful scenery, imagining myself in the canoe with Winnetou, or on a hunting expedition, or the warpath. This was my America, all open plains, rivers, woods, rolling hills, mountains. Everyone rode wild horses and spent their time traversing waterfalls in canoes. Franz and I were so smitten with it all that we actually built a canoe.

Some point out that May had to rely on other writers, since he did not visit the USA until late in life. Certainly I was to detect a familiar ring when I discovered Zane Grey's Wild West tales and my all-time favorite, James Fenimore Cooper's *Last of the Mohicans*; May was an avid reader of both authors. This does not bother me any more than Shakespeare reading Plutarch. I was hooked then and I intend to be again. As an adult I searched until I found a 22-volume set of May's works. When I retire I will reread them all, and with any luck they will bring back those golden days of youth.

We could not get enough of the latest in cutting-edge artistry, the Johnny Weissmueller Tarzan adventures. Cash flow problems were history once we discovered a hole in the back wall of the local movie theater, just large enough for us to crawl in beneath the stage, slipping up behind the curtain and through the darkness into choice front row seats. There was a catch—the seats were numbered, so we had to move when their rightful owners showed up—but this was a trivial price for a ticket to an endless film festival.

Marein life was not all fun and games. On top of schoolwork and reading there were household chores. My parents only planted half of our garden allotment, but that was 800 square feet, heaps of potatoes, cabbage, carrots, lettuce, beets, stringbeans, tomatoes, even a poppy patch. When the poppies ripened they had "pepper shakers", pods with seeds you could shake into your hand and eat by the handful. To us these seeds were for baking delicious poppy cakes. We had no idea poppies were used to make opium. No wonder we were always so cheery.

The other half of our allotment became a chicken and rabbit yard. We built cages for both and the rabbits lived up to their reputation as fast breeders. We fattened them up and had more than enough to slaughter one whenever we wanted a good meal. Similarly with the chickens, who also laid eggs for us every day. Nothing went to waste: chicken feathers disappeared into pillows and we cleaned, stretched and dried rabbit furs for the pelt dealer who came around every few weeks to buy them. No chicken escaped the coop in the morning until my mother's touch had personally verified it had at least one egg on the way.

Most people divided up their plots the same way, so the small camp sometimes looked like a cluster of miniature farms. It smelled like one too. To farmers like us this was a negligible price to pay for ample food, but it is just as well there was no room for pigs.

My job description included hoeing, weeding, slaughtering and skinning rabbits, gathering eggs, cleaning the chicken and rabbit coops and feeding the animals. As soon as I finished I was free, so I became very efficient and had plenty of time for soccer, adventures, berries and mushrooms. Also something new, something cruel.

Chickens include roosters, and boys being boys, roosters meant a new sport. "My rooster can beat your rooster" became a common boast. Breeding the biggest and meanest became everyone's hobby. There were so many cockfights that it ended up as an olympiad with systematic elimination rounds. Cocks take no prisoners, so every fight was to the bitter end. One owner walked away with the pot, usually money, and everyone else got death. None too Christian.

When the Stalzer pen produced the biggest rooster I have ever seen, we were sure we had a champion, but size proved a liability: it slowed him down and he was killed in his second fight. Our middleweight rooster, on the other hand, made it into the championship. Before each fight he was pure white; afterwards, white and red and blood all over. Small wonder this sport has been banned by most civilized nations.

In 1948 Richard and I joined dozens of other Camp 7 boys on a winter holiday at Eisenerz, an iron mining area in the mountains about 50 miles away. We stayed in a charming brick building nestled into a mountainside. This time the fashionable sport was not cockfighting but pillow fighting, so we got punished for making a mess rather than tormenting animals.

Far worse punishment was the ingenious warning against breaking the nighttime silence. They said one poor boy, whose name it would be mean to reveal, had the misfortune of being a sleepwalker. The full moon sent him wandering onto the roof, and at the slightest sound he would awaken and hurtle to his death. You have never seen a quieter dormitory. Fear of sharing the lost soul's curse had me hiding my head beneath the blanket whenever the moon shone through the window.

The real goal of this marvelous vacation was to fatten us up, and it succeeded. Except for the daily castor oil we were very grateful for the Austrians' obvious concern that our food please and nourish us. There were even inoculations against diseases like TB. Ironically, these failed to prevent a mumps outbreak, so those spared in earlier epidemics were able to catch up; but even they returned to camp looking and feeling much healthier.

The spring rains that year brought a bumper crop of the brown and white Portobello mushrooms we prized for their delicious taste and delicious sale price; also plenty of Pfifferlings, the small, clustered yellow mushrooms that tasted heavenly with scrambled eggs. Mushrooms were a lesson in the ambiguity of beauty: the most gorgeous was always the most poisonous. One red species with white polka dots poised its exquisite five-inch diameter on a delicate little stem surrounded with pretty rings. It beckoned like some vegetable Cleopatra, but we stole the visual bait without springing the fleshly trap. Naughty Mother Nature.

Business trumped pleasure again when six or eight of us headed up into an alpine valley for a high-stakes game of cowboys and Indians. One team had regular bows and arrows, the other crossbow-style rifles of our own invention: they shot a short arrow along a groove atop the barrel, using a heavy-duty rubber band strong enough to bring down small game. Blissfully ignorant of modern child safety protocols, we were chasing one another through the bushes in the ultimate war game when the whole pack of us burst into a clearing and surprised a young couple in the high grass. The lovers jumped up in complete panic. The young man was furious, imagining we had intentionally sneaked up on them; he grabbed a large stick and threatened to brain us, sending us scrambling for the exits.

We soon regrouped for a good laugh, but it did seem this might not be the ideal battlefield after all. Why not move to higher ground? Because as soon as we did we ran into a large gang of older Austrian boys. Here, miles from town, was their chance to teach the damned foreigners the true meaning of the word 'refugee'. As they came after us with their clubs we saw it would be stupid to stand and fight. Being no match for their size, we would have to capitalize on our speed and general fitness.

The starting pistol had fired and we were off. We had headstart enough to reach the first ridge before they could, and presence of mind enough to start rolling large boulders down at them, dislodging enough rocks and sand for a minor landslide. Suddenly we were not the only ones in serious danger. When they escaped into the trees to save themselves, giving us the crucial few minutes we needed to get away, we ran flat out all the way back to camp. Only then did we realize how lucky we were no one had been hurt.

There turned out to be far more net pleasure in the peaceful yearend bus trip the whole class of 1949 took up the mountain, at the scary edge of the narrow road with its spectacular panorama, winding up through the endless wildflowers. The bus pulled up to the alpine hut on the plateau and we spent hours exploring, interrupted only by a delicious box lunch, before it was time for group pictures at the bus and group singing all the way back down, led by the teacher and accompanied on the accordion by one of our classmates.

Those innocent pictures still touch my heart fifty-three years later. Despite the barracks, we had assimilated, we were free. We were "people without a country", yet full participants in Austrian customs and public festivities including the dozens of Catholic holidays from Advent to Whitsunday and Corpus Christi. Some occasions were too stuffy for kids, like the speeches accompanying the Labor Day parades on May First; others were fascinating but adults-only, notably Fasching, Carnival, which began on the 11th hour of the 11th day of the 11th month with parties running all the way through to the cosmic blowout on Rose Monday, just before Ash Wednesday. Every conceivable group had its own ball: pastry chefs, lawyers, florists, doctors, merchants, you name it. There were also balls for schoolchildren, even kindergartners, but as I suspected and later verified in Germany, they left out a few crucial grownup details.

A carny also came to town once a year, and luck landed me a job on the team propelling the space carousel. Six or so of us were up above on the platform, pushing the spokes of the turnstile that kept it revolving. People sat below us in baskets suspended on chains, and as we pushed and ran harder and harder they spun further and further out in space. Everyone had a blast except for the kids delivering the power. We were all nauseated with overexertion and some actually retched. Now we knew why it was so easy to get the job. As we collected our money we swore never to do it again.

Stench aside, the yearly circus was more pleasant and memorable. Many of the exotic animals we had never seen before: elephants, zebras, camels, giraffes, lions, tigers. And the death-defying acts and sideshows were so much more spectacular when you were not in the middle of them, turning green.

The most sentimental holiday was Mother's Day. Sentimentality is not always the same as kitsch; people who think this holiday an invention of the greeting card companies have not spent much time in Austria. The teachers spent weeks helping us with our handmade cards and our choice of wildflowers. Children competed to memorize poems for the public celebration in the town square, where we sang and bands played. We were delighted to display our appreciation for all our mother's good works, particularly her struggle when Papa was away. This was the special time to underline our respect for her plan in stressing positive outlook and determination, the can-do attitude that shaped our whole lives.

On Sundays the Austrian shops closed for more important business. We were active members of the 15th-century Catholic Church in Lorenzen. Like many of the local village churches, it was a miniature cathedral, replete with murals and statues, the inside walls beautifully tiled, the altar bright with gold and blooming with glorious weekly flower arrangements from the gardens of the lady parishioners. Sunday was High Mass and the special family moment of Communion. We learned the Latin using our parallel-text missals, Latin on the left and German on the right.

Christmas now began when the magical Christchild Markets opened during Advent, and carried through to Epiphany. In Austria and Germany you have Saint Nicholas instead of Santa Claus, and when they say he knows if you've been bad or good, they really mean it. He shows up on his day with his mischievous evil-spirit sidekick Krampus, and while the saint is giving presents to the good boys and girls, Krampus is lecturing the wastrels, even swatting them with a willow branch.

Naturally all the bigger boys loved to dress up as Krampus and terrorize the small children, sometimes beating them severely. When the Christmas spirit got completely out of hand there would be a war between the Krampuses, climaxing when the whole lot of them were surrounded by outside gangs and beaten up to avenge their victims.

Low buffoonery aside, our Christmas had been transformed entirely for the better. Where once the only sound had been the wind whistling through the slats as famished refugees huddled around the stove, you could now hear "Silent Night" caroled all through the camp on Christmas Eve. There would be no roast goose the next day, but would there not be special guests, a nice fat chicken, hours of sleigh rides? Poverty, where was thy sting? Affluence, where was thy victory?

Mama had made the traditional meal and we too had sung around the Christmas tree. Eleven o'clock was the time to bundle up and join the hundreds of people making their festive way to Lorenzen through the high snow, its frozen crystals glistening like diamonds beneath the moon and myriad stars, in the distance church bells and organ peals. Austrian and refugee alike found fellowship and peace sharing Christmas song and midnight mass. Sparklers illuminated the way home. It was the night of nights, the birth of the Messiah, the sign of His gifts.

The twelfth and last day of Christmas now saw kids going from house to house in groups of three, costumed, singing and reciting poems: the three Wise Men, Caspar, Balthasar, and Melchior, bearing the good tidings of Christ's birth. In return for a few cookies and chocolates, very occasionally a coin or two, we would write our initials C, B and M on the door as the Three Kings seal of approval.

For 1950 we received a milestone Epiphany present. Papa had decided the time had come to fill out the application for American citizenship. He explained that though there were strict quotas, we had made it across the first difficult hurdle. Our Uncle John in Smithtown had obtained firm job offers for Papa, Mama, and even Richard. With housing guaranteed by Uncle John, we could prove we would not be a burden on the state.

Our name went to the Gottscheer organizations in New York and from them to the Catholic Charities Organization for further sponsorship. The first step was taken; the long wait began. There would be plenty to learn meanwhile. Our Aunt Ida in New York had been sending regular packages of foods difficult to obtain in Austria, like coffee, sugar, and shortening, so I asked her if she could find me a football; we still played every chance we got, and we could never find decent balls. Having been imprudent enough to brag a real football was on the way, I was shocked when it arrived: an egg-shaped leather thing that bounced all over the soccer field and made me a laughingstock. Obviously the dictionary entry for 'football' left something out.

That June I graduated from grammar school with enough awards to join Richard in the Kapfenberg Junior High. Here there was little room for horseplay, and my perennial wiseguy streak got me in trouble even with the very nice Catholic priest who gave our religious instruction. One day he asked me a question and I gave what I thought was a very amusing answer. He thought otherwise and smacked me around until my ears rang. When I arrived home, my father immediately threw in a few for good measure, refusing to hear my explanation. If the priest whacked me, I must have done something bad. Since we had no telephone, I never could figure out how he had found out even before I arrived.

Real or imagined insolence was not the only possible felony. My math classroom faced on a ski jump framed by a gorgeous snow-covered mountain range, and watching the jumpers fly past the school often sent me into a reverie, soaring across virgin slopes, far from the dusty delights of mathematics. One day my mystical experience was rudely interrupted by an excruciating pain in my right ear. The teacher had conjectured that I could be returned to reality by a swift change in the angular momentum of my head relative to the blackboard. He explained in no uncertain terms that I was about to flunk out and had best start participating. I must have taken this to heart, as I seem to have passed with room to spare.

Indiscipline is more the colorful exception for someone raised in the university of wartime; at age 11, going on 40, I was pretty self-sufficient. In addition to our original businesses I had a lucrative new specialty: unearthing copper wire. One day we saw a multistrand cable poking its head from the ground outside a bombed-out factory. Digging led to a complete roll of lead-insulated cable, at least twenty strands of insulated wire, each strand neatly wrapped in paper.

A bonanza, but to be negotiable it would have to become anonymous scrap. We spent hours cutting short lengths and peeling away the lead, crumbling it to simulate a pile of junk. Then we stripped the remaining insulation and crumbled up the wires too. Voila, scrap. The junkyard gave me enough money to buy myself some real Austrian clothing. My image at school would never be the same. Speaking of school, I was now two hours late. Boy, was I in hot water.

Hotter still: my English teacher called on me to read my homework to the class. I had not done it. I explained that I had left it at home, but Mr. Mengler called my bluff. "Go get it."

How was I to walk to the railway station, catch a train to Marein, walk the remaining miles, do the work, and return, all in time to satisfy him? Simple: I sat down and worked at the station. Fortunately I also had the sense to kill time until the Marein train returned. Mr. Mengler had his suspicions, but I had done the work and he left it at that. Strictness was not an end in itself for this man. He knew we had our hearts set on America and he wanted me fluent enough to get by. It was tough love and I still thank him.

He could not have known that within months I would strike it rich, that in the space of a single minute I would go from struggling refugee to bourgeois. We would have the means to sail to America on a tourist visa. But until it was too late I would have no idea our problems were solved.

When I pulled my fortune out of the dump north of Lorenzen I thought at first it was a neat sword. Then I cleaned it: a noble, gleaming instrument, its handle adorned with brilliant stones. The curator of the Kapfenberg museum had a son in my class, so I brought it to school to show him. When he proposed taking it to his father, I insisted on coming along. No way was I just handing this thing over.

The curator marveled at a little boy presenting him a bejeweled late medieval sword. Then he threw me a curve ball. Would I consider donating it to the museum?

"Uh, yes, I suppose, of course, but—how much is it worth, anyway?"

"Well, a fair amount, I'm sure, but you know, the museum can't offer money. We rely on the generosity of collectors."

My better angel was satisfied, but the businessman in me needed to save face, and in my bracket a tax writeoff was not too enticing. Did they not perhaps have some copper and lead wire to make it an even trade?

They did. Now you know how the Indians lost Manhattan. The sword lived happily ever after at the Kapfenberg museum, and I was pleased to sell some more scrap. I had a long way to go as an art dealer, but I sure knew my scrap.

9

Hurry Up and Wait

This is the bag given to all refugees when they left Austria.

Hurry Up and Wait

The Marshall Plan was in full swing. The enormous US relief effort focused on rebuilding Europe, so rumors swirled about cutbacks in US citizenship programs for refugees: anyone who still wanted to make the cut would be well advised to accelerate their paperwork. Our relatives in America dropped everything to make the deadlines for recertifying our US home and job guarantees. We could remain optimistic, and my father began arranging for us to move closer to Salzburg, the camp where emigrants faced their final social and medical screening.

As soon as the school year ended we left Camp 7 for Camp 2, within walking distance of Kapfenberg. Richard had finished school and began his apprenticeship at the Böhler Works. We were all living in one room again, but we hardly minded, so little time remained before our trip to Salzburg and our ocean passage from Bremerhaven, Germany to New York.

English was my big focus when school resumed. Like most adult immigrants, my parents had scarcely learned a single word. They would be relying on Richard and me as interpreters and I was not about to let them down. All my teachers realized they had less than a year to prepare me, and they gave it their best, recommending books about America. I thought this superfluous, since Karl May had already informed me I was in for a great adventure, whitewater canoeing and riding up hill and down dale in the company of the noble red man. Was I ever in for a letdown.

Children were not the only ones with illusions about America. My English teacher had never been there, but some author had convinced him the dialect most likely to succeed in Brooklyn was "Oxford English", and he thoughtfully gave me extra tutorials to polish me for the dreaming spires of Flatbush.

Since Camp 2 was so close to Kapfenberg I could now walk to school again. The lovely road ran parallel to the Mur River, and we often dreamed of catching the large trout we could see swimming up and down in those curiously pristine days.

My emigration appetite was whetted when the Red Cross presented a movie about the Marshall Plan after school one day: boats and planes landing, unloading endless tons of food and raw materials in the largest relief effort ever, restoring the whole continent and Germany and Austria in particular. Such was the greatness and generosity of the American people, promising a wonderful life to anyone who landed on their shores.

Our applications had already been stamped and approved when immigration ceased abruptly in summer 1951. What had been a routine delay in the runup to

Salzburg became an agonizing wait. We had to wonder whether we had wasted all our hard work and shattered our own dreams by applying too late.

Adolf Schauer and other Gottscheer Relief Organization officials came to Europe to help break the deadlock. They paved the way for Gottscheers to receive 500 of the 5000 family vouchers the National Catholic War Council was prepared to provide. 500 families meant the Council would vouch for 2000 Gottscheers. The US recognized the special plight of Gottscheers who had all but fulfilled its requirements, and it agreed to finish processing all pending applications before slamming the gate shut. We had made it just under the wire; the DPC was dissolved August 31 and Gottscheer immigration more or less died with it.

We were jubilant with gratitude and itching with anticipation during the six months that elapsed before our Salzburg invitation arrived, instructing us to expect a month's stay.

One freezing January morning in 1952 the four of us boarded our train at Kapfenberg and set off westward through Bruck an der Mur. We climbed the mountains we had seen only from a distance, rolling along the entire range, through tunnels and the most beautiful landscapes I have ever seen, full of evergreens heavy-laden with snow, gleaming in the sunshine, well befitting a trek to the promised land.

An American Red Cross truck met us when we arrived after dark at Salzburg. More than twenty people crowded beneath the canvas cover. The cold was so dangerous that once again we had to press together for warmth. After an hour the gate of the processing camp emerged from the darkness. Naked streetlights in the narrow streets; barracks with a dozen or so double bunks in twin rows; heat from a central woodburning stove—except for the ban on cooking in the barracks it was a camp like any other, yet completely transformed by the knowledge that deliverance was at hand.

During the waits between the tests and consular interviews and physicals we were free to do some sightseeing. We took the streetcar to the old city center and explored the narrow side streets full of enchanting medieval houses and churches. Walking up to the ruins of the once-gigantic Salzburg Castle, we could overlook the entire city. We explored the catacombs below, where Christians once hid from the Roman armies that liked to toss them off the castle cliffs, and finally the wondrous cathedral and ancient cemetery at the base.

The first American soldiers we encountered were standing guard at a gas station in the center of the old city. When they saw Richard and me they beckoned us all over and very kindly gave us not only chewing gum and chocolate but also our very first bottle of Coca-Cola, which was just too novel for us. They laughed out loud when we made faces at the medicinal taste: how could little refugee kids not go for the American national drink?

As in other camps, the cold at Salzburg encouraged a flu epidemic. This caused a double delay, since you could not inoculate against other diseases until this one had run its course. Finally my parents were sent to the US Consulate for questioning. Who were our sponsors? What sort of jobs did we have lined up? What were our larger hopes? How did we picture America, and did we intend to become citizens?

My parents were well prepared and had no trouble convincing the consulate that they would be productive citizens. Their medical exams were also a breeze. Naturally it had to be me who caused complications.

The problem was that I had never been examined by a female doctor. I had faced air raids, Nazis, murder and mayhem, but never before had a beautiful woman demanded I drop my drawers. It was too terrifying. She had to remind me my visa was at stake before I would give in, turn my head and cough. Before I knew it the ordeal was over.

Several days later we were called in and given the green light, with all the necessary papers and visas. We were free to return to Kapfenberg and await instructions on when to report to Bremerhaven for final ship assignment.

We couldn't believe it. All that remained was to sell our belongings and watch the mailbox. The promised land was actually in sight. We were going to America. On the trip back to Kapfenberg even the glorious scenery could not completely distract us from our obsession with the upcoming voyage. Would we get seasick? What would New York be like? Would Uncle John be there to pick us up? The speculation was so engrossing that the trip seemed only five minutes long.

Papa set to work liquidating our things right away. This was no great challenge given that our worldly goods were limited to the two beds, the cooking stove, the pots and pans and bits and pieces of our one-room life at Camp 2. I did have a stamp collection, but there was no room, so I gave it to Franz. Even if we were better off we would not have been allowed to bring very much baggage, nor much cash. The plan was to get a little good clothing and have enough cash left over to buy food better than the notorious slop served to refugees at Bremerhaven. Buyers were there in no time and we were soon ready to move on. There was a unique excitement in the air as we notified the relatives to stop sending care packages and said our last goodbyes to the teachers who were so delighted for us.

My English teacher made me promise to send him an American Silver Dollar as soon as possible, a promise I was more than happy to make and later to keep.

The magic letter arrived in February. We were to report for final Bremerhaven processing March 20, with a tentative departure date of April 10. It was no use trying to concentrate until then; we could not focus on anything else. We did however experience unexpected twinges of buyer's remorse as the reality of our adventure hit home. After all, we had started to do pretty well here in Austria. Richard was an apprentice engineer. I was progressing just fine at school. Papa was a success at work and Mama was happy enough at home. They were 41 and 40 years old and were volunteering to start over from scratch in a language they did not speak.

Human nature has its absurdities. Once you have made a tough decision, you will never have to experience the downside of the road not taken, so looking back you can sometimes half imagine it was all upside. But on this one we all stood firm. The cards had been dealt only after careful planning. We were past the point of no return. Full steam ahead.

10

Crossing the Pond

The U. S. Navy Ship "SS General Stewart"

Crossing the Pond

We had forgotten that work expands to fill the time available. Much remained to be done before departure. Seven years in camp added up to more friends than we had realized, both refugee and Austrian, all wanting to stop by and bid us farewell. There were school arrangements, transcripts, deliveries of the belongings we sold.

When you are allowed little more than the clothes on your back, they had better be decent clothes. Richard and I used up our savings on the finest Austro-Bavarian suits, the expensive peak of fashion, stunning, dapper, and utterly inappropriate, setting us up for guaranteed ridicule from American kids.

Friends and family gave us a boisterous sendoff on the great day, March 17, 1952. We had plenty of help carrying our modest luggage to the Kapfenberg station. Papa was very nervous, checking and rechecking his pockets to ensure our papers were in order and our money safely stashed. Mixed feelings persisted even now: on one side, happiness and pride at making the grade; on the other, apprehension. Had we merely projected our "promised land"?

Doubts vanished once the steam locomotive set our adventure in motion. As it slowly pulled out we leaned far out the windows, waving to our friends, tears of both excitement and loss running down our cheeks as we pounded off around the bend into the far unknown. Then it was stops at Bruck an der Mur, Salzburg, Munich, with sublime peaks and landscapes in between. As night fell we dropped off to sleep, upright in our seats. Morning saw us pulling into Stuttgart, where Papa hopped off at the sight of a street vendor and brought us back a delicious treat of sausage sandwiches and sodas. On through Frankfurt, then Hannover on the second night, finally a two-hour stopover in Bremen for the final leg to Bremerhaven and the truck to the final processing center.

This was not your typical camp. Instead of wooden barracks there were brick buildings, possibly old military housing. With only a few people per room, it was a privacy upgrade. The lineups for the orientation lecture and the few remaining inoculations were almost a nostalgic goodbye to the queues of refugee life. The food did live up to its horrible reputation, but Papa reminded us we did not have to put up with it. We had budgeted for better rations all the way through the scheduled departure date. This proved particularly prescient; cash turned out to be altogether forbidden except for the five dollars issued each of us at boarding.

Off we went to explore the town and let the street vendors enjoy separating us from our money. Even on a careful budget there were many delicacies: sausages on bread, bratwurst with sauerkraut, irresistible cream cakes we returned for almost daily. We admired Papa for saving us from the soup lines others were forced to endure.

Sure enough, they picked us up very early on the appointed morning and delivered us to the docks, to the USS General Stewart, a magnificent old Army transport ship. Despite its drab Navy gray it seemed a luxury liner. A whole fleet of these transports had brought the American soldiers and sailors to Germany, and we were going to accompany some of them home from their European tours of duty.

They cut an exciting figure marching onto the ship with their duffel bags on their shoulders. Officers commissioned and non-commissioned shouted orders and the soldiers followed with brisk efficiency. It was as if they had staged a parade for our benefit. Once they were on board, those remaining were ordered to help us as we made our way up the gangplank, now and then looking back at the crowd on the dock.

The soldiers occupied the upper decks, so only the very bottom of the ship was left for the refugees. Arriving at our compartments, we found rows and rows of canvas bunks, three feet high with barely two feet of headroom. These would be our home for the next ten days on the high seas. We claimed our places and sat down to await further orders.

For each cabin the authorities designated a cabin boss as liaison and overseer. Ours was Papa. They gave him all the procedures, specific instructions and schedules. Every minute of the day was planned out, including a period after breakfast for the adults to clean the rooms while the kids went on deck. All thoroughly military, a tight ship.

Many of us were seasick within minutes of coming aboard. The ship had not even left port, but its gentle swaying in the harbor suffused the stuffy cabin air with nausea. We were in for a horrible ten days and we already regretted this whole affair. When the call came for lunch we were in no mood to eat, but we had to obey as they ushered us into the mess hall. The smell was unbearable, but we could see that objectively the food was good and the portions hearty, so we forced ourselves to eat.

A decisive jolt informed us the ship was moving. It headed west into the English Channel before the turn south into the Atlantic. The Channel was churning, with sizable waves, but the air on deck had settled our stomachs somewhat, so at first it seemed we might have some fun as the ship gently rode over each swell and the bow headed down into the next wave to drench us with spray. No such luck. After a few of these rolls there were dozens of people vomiting, most over the side but some right on the deck. I could keep most of my food down, but only in the fresh air, so I refused to return to the mess hall and my father had to bring my food to me on deck.

This merely postponed the inevitable. As we entered the Atlantic the seas grew so rough that we were ordered below. There was no choice but to lie in our bunks, swaying, bucking and in most cases vomiting. Only Papa stayed strong enough to escape the torment, and he managed to look after us all, bringing us food and drink and removing the half-processed results. Later we learned the Atlantic was always roughest from November through May. We had chosen the worst possible time to cross the pond, and I was sure we would die. What a way to end it all, after so much struggle.

Five monstrous days passed before the ship abruptly stabilized and we were allowed back on deck. We streamed up out of our hellhole into the chill brightness of a cloudless blue sky above waters as smooth as a mirror.

That day we were not the only ones who managed to keep some food down. After lunch someone cried out and we ran to the back of the boat to see what was going on. A school of swordfish and numerous large sharks were on our tail. It took us some time to figure out what this signified. They were dumping waste from the mess hall. It was the first time we had ever seen anyone throw away untainted food. Here they stood, feeding buckets and buckets of perfectly usable leftovers to the fish.

In our wake were also hundreds of those bitter green and yellow oranges they gave us every day. We could not bring ourselves to eat them. "When are they going to give us proper fruit?" Since we had never seen or heard of grapefruit, we thought they were failed oranges and did not realize we too were guilty of waste.

While the ocean remained calm we could visit the American soldiers on their upper decks. They were all very nice, giving us chocolates and Cokes. Being one of the few kids with a little English, I was instantly appointed interpreter. The GIs had also picked up a little German in Europe, and by throwing in lots of body language we could communicate most anything.

The ocean spoiled our conversation when it began churning furiously again and banished us below deck. Another five days, another five nights whose only constant was the urge to throw up. Somehow we learned Coke and saltines helped keep you from heaving, so they became valuable commodities through the night of the 19th, when light appeared at the end of the tunnel. We could go to sleep dreaming of the escape announced for the next day: our landing in New York.

11

First Impressions of Eden

The Statue of Liberty

First Impressions of Eden

In the end we did not sleep a wink. Anticipation alone was not enough to counter our nauseated depletion, yet there was a new buzz in the air as we hauled ourselves through our final luggage checks. This was the promised morning.

Each had his own vision of the promised land. For some it was skyscrapers and automobiles, good jobs and the prospect of riches. For others it was freedom, a place of one's own after the long years without a country. For me it was rolling plains, hills and mountains, the flora and fauna of the vast forests. My recurring dream of canoeing down the seething river had me so wound up with anticipation that it doubled my dizziness and nausea.

The ship had stopped rocking altogether and glided silently through the dense fog and drizzle that had disappointed the crowd on deck hoping for a clear vista. There were so many of us that when a cry went up from the port side, bringing everyone running to the rail, it almost seemed the boat would tip to the right.

What we saw made a profound impact, determining my whole future attitude about the United States of America. A majestic figure was emerging from the fog. It was the Statue of Liberty. In their jubilation people laughed and cried, danced and sang. We had been liberated. In a matter of hours we would reach the land of milk and honey, or so most of us thought; some cautioned there could still be plenty of hardships ahead. So greatly was I impressed with the Statue that I made up my mind then and there to join the US Army as soon as I came of age. My patriotism and love of my adopted country have grown every minute since.

Two tugboats joined the SS General Stewart as we passed the Statue, and began towing us toward the Brooklyn shoreline. Outlines of buildings began to appear along the docks, and suddenly we were gasping at the full New York skyline. I was stunned, overwhelmed. Quite a far cry from the Oregon Territory.

We had all seen Ellis Island in the movies and assumed we would be joining the hordes of immigrants and refugees that had entered there, but we now learned it had already closed down. We were headed for Fort Hamilton, Brooklyn, where one of the piers had been converted to a makeshift processing center; its gigantic proportions awed us as we docked.

Excitement was so high that we had to be directed aside so military personnel could disembark. A brass band played the National Anthem and "God Bless America" as the soldiers and sailors marched off the ship. The melodies stuck with me immediately, and as I hummed along I knew I would learn the words as soon as I saw them in print. Such feelings are so hard to describe that only those who have been there can really understand.

There was quite a scene as the refugees streamed off the boat with their meager belongings. Along the open dock were rows and rows of desks with volunteers and officials ready to admit us. Behind them was a high fence holding back a throng of people pressing to recognize their relatives, some of whom they had not seen in a great many years. My paternal Uncle John, who was coming to meet us with his wife Fanny, had been in the States for more than forty years and Papa had not seen him for thirty of them. This was the uncle whose three boys had fought the war on the US side, one of them dying in the Normandy invasion; we would soon be reminded how little love he had for Germany.

After half an hour my father and Uncle John spotted one another and were at least able to exchange greetings through the fence, but we still had to queue up at one of the desks for hours. The good news was that those with waiting relatives were free to go after they were questioned, their papers checked and their arrival recorded. As we waited we teased one another about the tags they had attached to us. 'TONY'—"to New York". Everyone called everyone else Tony. "This must be why so many Italian immigrants are called Tony."

For a long-lost brother Uncle John was unduly stern, unsympathetic and matter-of-fact. He immediately began spouting rules and regulations, rubbing it in that we were "greenhorns" with a lot to learn. He would speak and we would obey. This was an invitation for me to display my own hard-nosed attitude, which put me in Uncle John's doghouse almost the moment we met. I already knew I would be going my own way. The rest of the family might treat this man's word as law, but I had a specific plan of my own. I was not going to be a "greenhorn" for long.

He led us out of the port into the parking lot where his shiny new Buick was waiting. This was a very expensive automobile—he named a figure—and we earthlings were not to dirty it up. My father must have been impressed by this tactful reminder that he was a refugee with twenty dollars in his pocket to feed a family of four. Without Uncle John's bragging, how would we have remembered that we had nothing but the clothes on our backs?

The drive through Brooklyn deepened the bewildering gulf between my expectations and reality, but the greater the disorientation, the more intent I became on taking the American bull by the horns.

On our way to Smithtown in Long Island we stopped at Ridgewood in Queens to see Aunt Ida, whose son Karl had grown up with us. Ridgewood has always been a major Gottscheer stronghold, and our welcome in this pleasant two-story house was 1000 percent heartier, befitting a lady who had so generously sent care packages all those years. She was overjoyed to see us, regretting only that Karl still had a few weeks to go before coming home from the Japanese hospital where he had overcome his Korean War wounds.

Aunt Ida had prepared a fantastic feast, but I still could not bear even the smell of food and they had to park me on the living room sofa with a pail on the floor beside me. My first exposure to television: filling the pail while the circus paraded gaily across the screen and unintelligible streams of excited conversation percolated in from the dining room through the miasma of nausea.

In mid-afternoon the stentorian voice of Uncle John cut things short. It was still two hours to Smithtown and he did not care for nighttime driving. Staying with Aunt Ida would have been much more pleasant, but it was Uncle John who was sponsoring us. However Americanized he might be, he still acted more Prussian than Gottscheer. Forget orientation; this was Sunday, so Mama and Papa reported for work tomorrow morning.

Thirty minutes into the carsick drive I announced I could not hold it in a second longer. Uncle John instructed me to hold it in anyway. One didn't just pull off the parkway. Whatever you say, Uncle John: up it came, all over the back of his seat, sealing my fate. Suddenly he was able to pull off the parkway.

The hour had come for my introduction to American curses. I heard "little bastard" as he mopped up, and many other colorful terms, all the way back to Smithtown. Every one of those words echoed in my memory and was translated the moment I got my hands on a dictionary. They poisoned our relations for the rest of his life.

12

Cry Uncle

Uncle John's house on Meadow Road, between Kings Park and Smithtown, Long Island. The garage became our home.

Cry Uncle

Uncle John had a little house on a little hill, on ten acres off Meadow Road, half-way between Smithtown and Kings' Park. The narrow kitchen had the formica table and plastic-covered metal chairs of the era. Next to the kitchen, the living and dining rooms were a single space with a room divider. There was one small bathroom and three tiny bedrooms.

My parents' bedroom had a bed and dresser, but Richard and I had to share a mattress on our floor for several months. Uncle John thought this fine for 'green-horns', but it was confining, fancy only by comparison with our former environment. Had we entered a glorified refugee camp? Not me. I was busting out at the first opportunity. My parents had different plans too. They knew we would not live this way for long if we pursued the true American dream.

On that first morning Uncle John dropped Mama and Papa off at their job. They were laborers in a commercial laundry on the wrong side of Smithtown, but they did not particularly mind. So long as there was a paycheck the work ethic would see them through with dignity. What startled us was that Americans are not guaranteed health insurance. If you fall ill you are on our own. Calling this a letdown would be an understatement. At least Austria had health care.

Lest he lighten our burden, Uncle John never let a day go by without telling us what a sacrifice he had made to get us to America. What was his problem? He had led us to believe he wanted us to come.

When Aunt Fanny took Richard and me to Smithtown High for registration, she stopped in front of Town Hall to point out the name "Rudy Stalzer" proudly displayed on the monument to fallen soldiers. His name was also displayed in the school. Rudy was one of about twelve young local kids who enlisted in World War II and never returned.

The first day of school was utter consternation. Teenagers can be cruel herd animals, and we were obviously the odd men out, highly suspect. Just look at us with our Austrian clothes, our meager English, our British accents. One girl actually approached me to ask whether I was a Nazi. This was not going to be easy.

When Aunt Fanny picked us up from school I asked whether we could stop by a bookstore and pick up a German-English dictionary. This she was kind enough to do, and it immediately became my constant companion. From the very first day I memorized six English words every night and made a point of using them throughout the next day, even if I had to twist the context.

She underlined that she would not be chauffeuring us after the first day. Fair enough. We would wait for the school bus, and if we missed it we would have to walk the four miles to school.

That first afternoon after school was our first chance to explore outside the house. Behind the large two-car garage were the remains of a long chicken coop. The backyard gave on an orchard; beyond were the woods that became my constant haunt. I found a BB gun in the old chicken coop and Uncle John reluctantly said I could keep it so long as I did not use it near the house. The many hours I spent hunting for squirrels and rabbits were also handy for getting away from my uncle, but he did make sure I performed my assigned chores, such as mowing the grass with a hand mower and sweeping the driveway. The woods also yielded extra-large blueberries, though I was reluctant to eat them at first because they had white fruit inside instead of being blue all the through.

By the time we settled into our rounds of bus, school, and chores, the kids had started in on us, shoving us and calling us original names like "Nazi". My first-round fistfight was on the third day of school. A boy took me by surprise when he came up to me and pushed me hard, showing off for his friends. I staggered and tripped flat on my back. He had not reckoned on me jumping up, diving at him and wrestling him to the ground, where we were still rolling when the teacher pulled us apart.

This became a daily routine. They pushed me, I pushed back. They punched me, I punched back. I was not about to play the victim; my brother, on the other hand, did not have a single fight. He simply refused. When they pushed him, he walked away.

One afternoon I boarded the school bus home sporting a bloody nose and a black eye. The three boys behind me looked just as bad; I had managed to give as good as I got. My brother was waiting for me at the back of the bus: "Well, you did it again, didn't you." I retorted that my bloody nose did not hurt half as much as he was hurting inside. Turning the other cheek can be costly.

After a few weeks the attacks began to subside. Like most bullies, they were giving up once they figured out I would hurt them back. Their new sport was to test my strength, which was not inconsiderable after the tough workout of the past seven years. Someone would say "Hey, Stalz, let me give it a try", and the boys would all line up behind me to try twisting my arm behind my back. I would lock my elbow and stick out my arm. One by one they tried to twist it behind my back. One by one they failed.

This spawned a truce of sorts. Though they did not particularly like me, they decided I was OK and even invited me to play softball with them. I had no idea what to do. When I was 'up', they led me to the plate and I tried to imitate their movements, swinging wildly. Beginner's luck sent the ball over the fence, the first of several random home runs that day. I was a lousy player, but I was powerful, so if I happened to connect it was siyonara.

Aunt Fanny was always admonishing us not to say much to the other students. "They don't like Germans." Above all we should keep our opinions to ourselves when the class had its mock presidential election. This was the land of the free?

I voted for General Eisenhower. Wasn't he German?

My favorite period was wood shop. Watching my father handle wood all those years had given me a knack for woodworking, and in shop there was no need to talk. My other forte turned out to be watercolors, both still life and landscapes.

Richie and I had been using a small Ehler's coffee can as a piggy bank ever since our arrival in Smithtown. Visiting relatives invariably contributed a handful of loose change. When it was full enough to dump the contents on the floor, to count our booty and familiarize ourselves with the various denominations, we found everything from pennies to half-dollars. The dime was an anomaly, the only coin that did not state its value in cents. This inspired me to propose a naughty trade: I would give Richie one big juicy nickel for every five puny, anonymous dimes. It took Richie days to realize he had been had, but once he did he petitioned for redress of grievances, smacking me and demanding a refund.

By the end of April I had made my one and only friend, a kid by the name of Benny, with the German family name Budelmann, who lived half a mile down the road. Like Franz with his library, Benny took me under his wing for a crash course in the American Way of Life. While my uncle was most inhospitable, forbidding us any guests, I was always welcome at Benny's house. His mother Sofie and his two sisters were invariably gracious. Joan, the elder, was Venus in the flesh; Helen too was cute, but unripe enough to spare me the secret torments of bootless longing. We spent many hours together, enjoying lunch and TV, and one Sunday they even invited me to join them on their weekly pilgrimage to the grave of Benny's biological father.

Benny's stepfather was a retired railroad man, still so in love with trains that he built a model railroad large enough to carry children, with a real steam engine and five cars. It appeared in a number of movies. The track ran all the way around the house, and on any given day you could see Benny's stepfather playing conductor for the neighborhood kids.

By the end of the school year in June I was fairly well acclimated. Reciting the Pledge of Allegiance and singing the National Anthem every morning had made me quite patriotic, and I thoroughly enjoyed the prospect of citizenship. The kids at school realized that I was not a Nazi and stopped excluding me. They found out I could be quite useful with difficult math problems: although my age bracket had landed me in the sixth grade, I was far ahead in math, science and geography.

Richard joined my parents at the laundry; my uncle had browbeaten him into leaving school at sixteen. "You don't need more education, get to work and help cover these bills, you're old enough." I scorned Uncle John for this and was once again accused of "trying to be a big shot". The best I can say for him is that the more I saw of him and his dropout sons, the less tempted I was to waste my chance at school.

Uncle John had a nefarious master plan for us. He told my parents he had a building permit to convert the garage into a small apartment. Since he was a carpenter, he could do most of the framing and my father the finishing. We could rent there, but only if we paid for the entire project.

My father was delighted to play along, since getting out of the house was worth plenty. Everyone saved every penny they could: except for housing my father never bought anything unless he could pay cash up front. Even we were amazed when he announced he already had enough for the refrigerator and stove. By the time the apartment was done, the kitchen and bedroom furniture was paid for as well.

Between regular chores and the apartment, free time was tighter that summer, but Benny and I still found many hours to explore the forests around Meadow Road. It was almost a chapter out of Karl May. We went hunting and fishing deep in the woods, building rafts to float down a small stream. He introduced me to the town pool, and when he got a summer job in the local movie theater he smuggled me in several times for my beloved Johnny Weissmueller Tarzan adventures.

It was at the movies that I first found puppy love. Joyce, blonde and petite with a wonderful smile, politely oblivious to my drooling, but hopelessly out of reach: what would a beautiful and intelligent girl see in a refugee with barely enough English to top Tarzan? The captain of the football team soon picked up the scent and I was history.

Construction resumed every day right after work. The biggest task was digging the enormous cesspool by hand. It had to be at least 15 feet in diameter and almost as deep. Richard and Papa did the digging with pickaxes and shovels, while I wheeled the dirt into the woods and filled ditches with it.

Uncle John did a respectable job of framing out the garage and the rear bathroom extension. His pals did the plumbing and electrical work and we soon had two little bedrooms, a small kitchen with a little breakfast nook, and a generous bathroom. Papa had the furniture delivered as soon as the paint was dry. It was a proud moment: he owned everything but the structure itself free and clear. By September the construction materials were paid for and we could move in. Rent started coming due right away, but the sensation of ownership was fun while it lasted.

When Cousin Karl returned from Korea, the first thing he did upon visiting us in Smithtown was take me to a clothing store for some American outfits. What a rush to be back in school all decked out in nice cotton shirts and slacks. The kids saw The Refugee quite differently. I was one of them.

That semester introduced us to some classic small-town Americana beginning with a fantastic Fourth of July parade. Marching bands, baton twirling, Shriners, the lot. Football started in September and the cheerleaders let me hang out with them during practice and at the games. Then there was Halloween, when Smithtown kids sneak over to slap bright red paint on the pizzle of the large bull statue at Jericho Turnpike and Meadow Road. The law forbids this, but neither the police nor the amused pedestrians would dream of interfering with hallowed tradition.

Just when we thought life had started to be kind, Uncle John dropped the real bomb. He had decided to sell his property. "I'm getting older and I need to be closer to town. Besides, this place is getting too big for me to keep up." This just two months after construction. My father pleaded with him to hold on a year or two until we could buy it, but he was deaf to all entreaties. Even a child could see the injustice had to be premeditated. Thanks to our free capital and slave labor our magnanimous uncle's assets had appreciated tidily, thank you very much. My father was distraught at being cheated by his own brother, but I had no illusions to lose.

Where were we to go? The boss at the laundry liked the family and did not want to lose us, so he offered to find us another apartment in town. Karl lobbied for Ridgewood in Brooklyn. It was a Gottscheer stronghold, closer to the rest of the family; and it was the knitting capital of America, with plenty of employers hungry for the Gottscheer work ethic. He was right on all counts. It was he who found us a place, and except for me everyone found a job. The old question marks resurfaced as I contemplated changing schools yet again.

Needless to say, my father had very little contact with his brother after we moved out. Only years later did we find out the end of the story, more proof that what goes around really does come around. Our garage apartment had burned to the ground, supposedly an electrical fire. In succumbing to Uncle John's wiles we had cheated the reaper.

13

The Dukes of Brooklyn

Public School #162—Willoughby Junior High, Brooklyn, N.Y. 1954

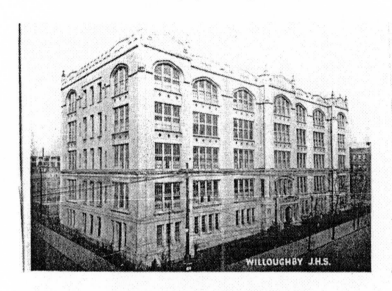

The Dukes of Brooklyn

The movers came first thing. It took little time to load our belongings onto the truck, but surveying them with the eyes of Camp 5, we had reason to be pleased with our progress. There was the stove, the refrigerator, a nice formica kitchen set with a table and four chairs, and two whole bedroom sets. My parents' was a queen bed with box spring and mattress, two side tables, two night lamps, and two dressers. We boys had twin beds, also with box spring and mattress and matching night tables and lamps.

The dealer had thrown in all the lamps as a bonus when we bought the sets. It was the sort of moment parents love but do not always spot as they fly by: the satisfied, proud expression on my father's face left a permanent imprint on me as he expounded the cardinal rule of economy. "Look at this, we paid for all this in cash, it's a done deal. Some of my co-workers are still making payments on their furniture."

Our uncle's anticlimactic performance had revitalized the core Stalzer attitude and our perennial motto: turn your stumbling blocks into steppingstones. My parents had taught us we could always transcend setbacks if we just put our heads down and went back to work; and once we chose Ridgewood we were back in the game, putting into play the hand fate had dealt.

Piling into the car, we followed Karl down the hill. We still noticed each new street in as much detail as we noticed each new acquisition, and tried to find something positive though our hearts were sinking as the lovely trees and meadows of Long Island deserted us. The absurd thing was that I had finally mastered the Smithtown High song, just as the school was yanked out from under me. I must have sung it a dozen times before we hit Brooklyn:

> Smithtown High holds mem'ries fond
> Friendships tried and true
> May our Mem'ries ever come
> Back again to you.
> Lift your voices, Seniors, Juniors,
> Sophomores, Freshmen too,
> Hail to thee, our alma mater,
> Hail, all hail to you.

From Meadow Road it was Jericho Turnpike and a right turn west, down the Northern State Parkway and the Interstate Parkway, off through Forest Hills. Stores and apartment buildings, warehouses and schools. Metropolitan Avenue was the last leg to Brooklyn and we noted Wyckoff Heights Hospital as we passed. One last left and we were home, at 212 Wyckoff Avenue.

Life had posted us to the middle of a long block of attached four-family and eight-family houses in dire need of repair. You could see the elevated train two blocks away. The people on the street looked like us: poor. They milled around to sniff out the newcomers and we soon saw we would be among mainly Italian immigrants. The Gottscheer neighborhood was within walking distance, but Karl had not been able to find anything affordable there.

We were on the second of four floors above the cutlery shop owned and run by our landlord. At the landing we encountered a door marked "Toilet". This we would have to share with the people across the hall. Just like old times, but without the snowdrifts.

Entering the apartment, you had to turn left into the kitchen. You could see the first room beyond it but not the next two. Now we knew why it was called a railroad apartment: to get to the back rooms you had to barge through the front of the train. Mama and Papa got the privacy of the last room, Richard and I the next, and the room adjoining the kitchen became the living room.

The next little surprise was that this was also a cold water flat. The only water was one lonely faucet, a washbasin in the far corner of the kitchen. To get hot water you had to fire up a gas stove. There was no exhaust, so inattentiveness could mean carbon monoxide poisoning; each day the paper reported some new family found dead after leaving the stove on to keep warm at night.

We got busy installing the stove and positioning the refrigerator. The table and chairs went into the center of the room and presto, our kitchen was complete. Once the bedroom sets were in we had a semblance of a home. Within a few weeks we had saved for a living room set too. Primitive? Maybe, but freedom from Uncle John's constant scrutiny was civilization in itself.

The first order of business was to restore cash flow. Mama went straight back to work in a commercial laundry, Papa and Richard at a carpentry workshop in Jamaica, joining Uncle Andrew, the husband of our maternal aunt. They had arrived in Brooklyn from the refugee camps just a few months ahead of us.

I earned my two-dollar allowance taking care of the grocery shopping, dishwashing and garbage. It barely sufficed for my school supplies and clothing, so before long I had a job at Weiss's Fruit and Vegetable Store two blocks away. Now my parents only had to cover my food and shelter. Another return of the spiral, up and around to the virtual self-sufficiency of my scrap iron days.

The principal at Smithtown Junior High had given me a letter to deliver to Willoughby Junior High on St. Nicholas Avenue, about two miles away. Money was too tight to take the city bus down Wyckoff Avenue. Essentially I would have to register myself, since Mama and Papa had no English, but Mama came along in case they needed her signature. This was my debut as the family's official interpreter and travel agent: for years I saw to it that Mama and Papa knew where they were going and what people were saying when they got there.

At first we were surprised the Willoughby principal received us so warmly, but it turned out the Smithtown principal had called to introduce us, saying he was not sure what grade I really belonged in. Since I had just finished the seventh grade with flying colors, Willoughby took an unusual gamble and placed me with the eighth-graders for the remaining two months of their term. It paid off; even here I was strangely ahead of the game in math, geography, handwriting and science. The anomaly was resolved when Willoughby contacted my school in Kapfenberg and got a clearer idea of Austrian standards. In June they graduated me from the eighth grade.

They would not be disappointed. Nothing was going to stop me from excelling. My linguistic principal of six words a day continued to accrue compound interest and I aced every math challenge presented me at the blackboard, even where I could not explain the method abstractly. My 92 average landed me at the top of my class, number three across all ninth-grade classes, and my parents had the satisfaction of seeing my name in the yearbook.

Graduation meant transfer to Bushwick High on Irving Avenue, in one of Brooklyn's toughest neighborhoods. The movies of that period do not lie; gangs and rebels without a cause were facts of life. Jimmy Dean, Sal Mineo, Natalie Wood—the stars drew their light and fire from the real-life volcano of postwar adolescence. Willoughby had given me a solid introduction to the mean streets; the informal social studies curriculum included confrontations both in and out of school. Where Smithtown violence had been strictly one-on-one, here it was more often gangs, with one exception that has proved more unforgettable than the rule.

All Willoughby groaned under the iron rule of a gang of Italian punks who loved to intimidate the other kids and push them around. I had come to the particular attention of a certain Mario. He had repeatedly baited me, but I had held my fire. It was a trap. Only the presence of his friends made him cocky enough to challenge me, and if I fell for it the whole lot of them would attack me, falsely claiming I had picked on a smaller boy.

But the day came when Mario sauntered right up to me during a study hall period in the auditorium and got in my face with the whole world watching. He whipped out a piece of licorice, ostentatiously dropped it to the floor and ground it in with his shoe. Grinning and surveying the crowd, he loudly declared war. No one present could fail to hear his taunt—"Here, Nazi, eat this"—as he shoved the filthy licorice through my lips.

That did the trick. Sorry, but he was playing with gasoline. My self-control and diplomatic calculation blew straight out the window. Picking him up, I heaved him over my head and hurled him across a row of seats. The whole room fell silent and I had a brief eternity to contemplate the scary possibility I had broken his back. Thankfully his friends managed to help him get up and stumble away, in obvious pain. You could feel the tacit verdict of approval throughout the relieved auditorium. No one had yet had the nerve to confront these jerks. I even reaped a few conspiratorial winks, though no one yet dared be seen congratulating me.

When the dust settled, a German immigrant prudently masquerading as a gang sympathizer discreetly tipped me off that—they—would be lurking out front after class to beat me up. In my adrenaline rush I pegged him for a plant, aiming to manipulate me into going out the rear door where there would be no witnesses to the ambush. In fact his tip was clean. There were at least six of them out front, characters straight out of "Grease": jeans, T-shirts, garrison belts, leather jackets.

Word of a rumble had spread and the audience was packed. I must have been the only one entirely ignorant of protocol in these matters of state. Feigning nonchalance with all my might, I ambled absentmindedly homewards, across from the crowd shouting "rumble, rumble". They followed all the way to Wyckoff Avenue, where the gang abruptly materialized around me, thrusting Mario at me, his fist blasting deep into my left eye.

Even as I saw stars I was coming back at him. There was no walking away from this one. The battle was joined; worrying about the war would have to wait. As little as I relished a match with a smaller boy, they had to know I meant business. When I plowed into him, fists blazing, it was over in seconds. He could barely hold back his tears as the encircling gang witnessed his prostrate disgrace.

Round Two was mine, and I seized the moment to cut through the circle and continue home, wondering what would come next. The gang followed, brandishing knives and threatening to "cut me up". Still playing it cool, just looking over my shoulder now and they in case they jumped me, I soberly removed my garrison belt and wrapped it around my knuckles. The buckle could split a head in half if used as directed.

A block went by, then another. No attack, just a barrage of terrible threats lest I dare reappear at school. They ended up escorting me all the way to my door, which I slammed in their faces without looking back. What a relief, and what a scary prospect for the next day.

When the family returned from work and saw the black eye and bruised knuckles, they wanted to walk to school with me the next morning and enlighten the principal. I would have none of it. Showing up with my father and brother would just reveal that I feared for my life.

The family had enough confidence in me to let me go it alone, but the next morning I took a deep breath as I headed off to school. This was going to be a make-or-break day. All eyes were on 'Stalz' as I arrived in the schoolyard, still exuding fearlessness, still petrified. Walking over to the wall, I took out my pink rubber ball and went into my usual morning handball routine. Within sixty seconds someone grabbed me by the shoulder and spun me around. Mario's buddy, spitting in my face. By the time the teacher intervened we had tumbled all the way across the concrete terrace, kicking and punching. The war was on, and it seemed it would be Stalz versus all comers: not one person was coming to my aid.

When the bell rang, Mario and I were summoned to the gym teacher's office. "I hear you two are having a rumble? Well, we're going to settle this once and for all. We're going to the gym and you guys will put on gloves and duke it out." The chastened Mario replied "not me", and walked out.

That day no one followed me home. I changed and reported for work as usual at Weiss's. At dusk it was time to bring in the fruit and vegetable crates used for sidewalk display. As I walked around the corner between loads someone yelled: "Hey, Stalz". Looking up I saw four gang members sitting on one of the parked cars. They were playing with switchblades, as conspicuously as possible.

Great. How was I going to get home tonight? I had to tell Mr. Weiss what was going on. He was not fazed, saying in his thick Jewish accent: "Don't worry, I'll take care of this". Hiding behind his back the long knife he used for watermelons, he walked slowly out of the store and around the corner. When he was about ten feet from the kids he brandished it with a sudden scream, charging them and swinging it like a machete. Taken totally by surprise, they sprang from the car and hightailed it down the street. Alice in Wonderland: wiseguy personas shattered by a man little more than five feet tall.

This was clearly a temporary fix. The teachers had been alerted, and several days passed in an uneasy truce, but there were verbal threats throughout the day. They would be back.

At least there was no school on Saturday, the day I did home delivery of fruits and vegetables. That evening I was coming out of a dark alley, counting my change and tips, when I bumped straight into a giant. Or so he seemed, towering over me at about 6'6".

"Hey, kid, do you know Mario?"

"Mario who?" I replied, but he was in no mood for games. He set into me with both fists, beating me to a pulp. I could hardly drag myself back to the store. This goon turned out to be Mario's big brother, home on leave from the Marines. Mario, true to form, had claimed I had beaten him up for no reason.

After a drubbing like that even a grown man feels he has little left to lose, and to my fifteen-year-old mind the feud was taking on eschatological overtones. It was time to finish Mario off. When I hit school on Monday, I looked like meat grinder residue but inside I was granite and steel. Mario was in the schoolyard with his friends, all poking fun at me, rubbing salt in my wounds: "Hey, Stalz, did you fall off the elevated train?" Their laughter gave out plenty fast when I charged them. There must have been murder in my eyes, because they scattered like deer and Mario ran for his life. The tables were turned and it was his turn to tremble. All the way through graduation, I went after him no matter where I saw him, and he seemed to sense he might well die if I caught him.

Standing up to this gang and living to tell the tale had made me something of a celebrity. Kids started to befriend me; I even fell head over heels for one Amelia Bayer, the cutest Italian girl imaginable, petite, with jet black hair and a brilliant smile. I thought about her every time I heard the Bayer Aspirin commercial. It seemed mutual, but when the semester ended, so did our infatuation; she transferred to another highschool. Six or eight years later I bumped into her on Wyckoff Avenue, married, with four chubby kids, so fat that I hardly recognized her. You figure.

I ran into Mario, too, when I got out of the Army in 1960. The gang had never come after me again; maybe they split up that summer when so many kids went away. But when our eyes met on Myrtle Avenue it was instant recognition. The time had come to shake hands and share a laugh at the folly of youth. I started walking over, but he panicked and bolted. I must have been a more imposing rumbler than I imagined, back in the olden days. Much later I learned he had spent years in and out of jail.

14

Age of Gold, Age of Iron

James Dean? No, The Stalz under the "E1" on Myrtle Avenue

Age of Gold, Age of Iron

Business turned pleasure in the summer of 1954, when I landed a job as full time carrier for the Long Island Press. The home office was on Myrtle Avenue at Menahan Street, right under the elevated train; half the time we had to shout to be heard. Weekdays I picked up my papers in the afternoon; Sundays it was 4 in the morning, and all the extra comics and ads made the paper so heavy that those of us with larger routes had to return and reload numerous times.

For my brand new job my father took me to the bike shop and bought me a brand new bike, to which we added an enormous front basket. The District Manager, Bill Bauer, gave me a few hours of training and accompanied me on my first rounds. Holding my delivery list against my bike handle, I followed his car to Knickerbocker Avenue and Starr Street, which turned out to be one of the toughest neighborhoods even in Bushwick. These streets bordered Knickerbocker Park, which teen gangs turned into Rumble Central after school, sometimes well into the night.

I began with about 65 customers, but the stationmaster was always prodding us to increase our base. "You are doing the trip already. With just a little more effort you can deliver a lot more papers." I purchased five or ten extra papers per day on my own account, as free samples to whet the appetites of prospective customers.

My method was foolproof. Since I always started at the same time of day, soon I could tell exactly where on my route I would be in any five-minute period. Each customer could count on his paper almost like clockwork. This let me go to the neighbors not yet signed up and make them a special offer. First came the standard pitch. "I will deliver this paper for a full week free, no obligation. If you are satisfied with my service, I hope you will sign up for 13 weeks." Then came the closer. "Your paper will arrive at this time every day, rain or shine, or it will be free." The prospects could not resist seeing whether the kid was up to the challenge, and I signed up ninety percent of them, becoming the top salesman in the entire office. This meant not only better commissions and tips but all kinds of prizes: Thanksgiving turkeys, another bike, even a cash bonus for new territory. By the time I quit to take a 'real' job in my senior year at Bushwick, my route was 260 papers, forcing me to subcontract subroutes to two other boys. I had also been kicked upstairs to stationmaster, taking management overrides on the whole delivery force.

This gig was great for my savings account, but it did present me a few more stumbling blocks to transform into steppingstones. If I wanted to maintain my reputation for punctuality, I could not afford to stop even for my Friday pay-check: there were so many Friday papers that some new subscribers already had to wait until Saturday for theirs. The extra tips for the extra care more than made up for a day's delay in base pay.

At Christmas the other carriers inserted a holiday card into each paper. This was too impersonal for me. I wrote every card, addressed the envelope, tacked on a four-cent stamp. Every customer received one in time for Christmas. This paid major dividends. On average I already collected two to three times more tips than the other kids, and Christmas meant up to three dollars more per customer. By the time I laid off on December Fridays and Saturdays I could have been Santa; the entire inside of my shirt was bulging with dollar bills wrapped in Christmas cards.

One Christmas a man stopped me in the driveway of a house where I had just collected. "Hey, kid", he said in a menacing voice, "hand over the money".

Street Zen had me shoving my mechanical pencil into his gut so instanta-neously that he could well have thought it an expert knife. "Get lost, buster, or I'll cut you wide open." And in the next breath: "help, help, holdup!" Who says no cry but "fire" will bring people to your rescue? The door behind us jerked open and out came my customer, baseball bat at the ready over his head. The mugger hauled his sorry carcass out of there faster than Jesse Owens, and I had a volunteer bodyguard for the last few deliveries.

True customer service is the soul of good business, and it includes followup. When I got home I dumped all the cards onto the kitchen table and made careful note how much loot each customer had provided. Each one had a custom thank-you note inserted in their next paper.

Chronic stumbling block #2 was the kids who were always trying to pick fights with me during my rounds. Necessity forced me to invent the rumble post-ponement. "Look, I can't get into this right now, but I'll meet you in Knicker-bocker Park at eight o'clock tonight."

The first kids I tried this on were so astounded that they laughed and walked off, saying "Sure, Stalz. If you don't show up, we'll kick your a—." They were sure I was weaseling out, but I was well aware that if I did they would keep their promise and ambush me on my route. They were nonplused when I showed up right on time.

These fights were mostly for show; they were all trying to sign me up for their gangs. Their childish mentality wanted everyone filed under some gang tag, but in the end they had to accept my insistence that I would rather be a loner.

The Stalz gang of one became the talk of the neighborhood. "Challenge Stalz, he'll show up." The postponement method cost me more than one bruise, bloody knuckle and bloody nose, but it kept my business healthy. Not a happy arrangement, but better than getting beaten up every day, and respect-inspiring enough to keep most of my showdowns one-on-one. The gangbangers stood aside until it was over, like spectators at a wrestling match.

Only one other kid ever fought beside me: a fellow Gottscheer carrier, Joe Schmidt. Joe was not as fanatical as I about timing his route, so he could make time to come along when a big storm was brewing. Together we became a two-man infantry. Everyone knew he was deadly with the nine-foot bullwhip he wrapped around his handlebars, and he was the type that really enjoys the rough stuff. He ended up joining the Army and going Airborne.

That summer I met Adolf, a brand new Gottscheer immigrant whose parents had opted to stay longer in Klagenfurt after the war. 'Adi' made me feel like an old hand at the American Way of Life. Somehow those six words a day had become six thousand, and it was up to me to show him the ropes. I took him under my wing and brought him into my circle of friends, including the soccer team in Highland Park. Thus began a friendship that was to last throughout our lives, through the Army and every personal triumph and tragedy.

Adi preferred playing goalkeeper. During a practice game he was charging out of the goal to block one of the onrushing opponents when he slid into him and we heard a loud crack, followed by a shriek of agony. Everyone laughed at the ragdoll pose he struck, but the sound had been his leg breaking in two places, and within moments it dawned on us that he needed to rush to the hospital. The trainer helped him get up on his good leg and hop to the car.

I was left with two bikes, mine and Adi's. At first it seemed I would have to resign myself to walking both of them all the way to Ridgewood; but I discovered I could ride mine and hold his by the handlebar. His parents were most grateful when I arrived at Gates Avenue with the story, and there was a surprise bonus to follow.

The welcoming committee at Adi's hospital consisted of four girls who were not only pretty but also insistent on hugging and kissing me. A social experiment by the State of New York? No, these were Adi's grateful cousins, the Wolf girls. Edith, the second youngest, was a beauty with a Texas-size smile and I took an immediate, blissful shine to her. The cousins were home for a week from their summer house on Long Island and would soon depart again until the fall, so our meeting was a fluke, but it was good for a whole summer's worth of dreams.

Adi's leg mended very quickly and he was able to man his goalpost sometimes in the fall, but it was some time before he could abandon caution enough to be suitably aggressive. Meanwhile, he had more time for accordion practice.

In a sense that fall was the beginning of manhood, my first major departure from family consensus. Everyone was telling me to quit school and go to work, since I already had the best education in the house. In our family the question of college did not arise; even graduating from high school was a lofty goal, but I could not resist the challenge. My solution was to finish school on the commercial rather than the academic track, learning sten, typing and bookkeeping with a view to an office position.

My guidance counselor made sure I took enough academic credits to keep the college option open, and this was fortunate, but so was inadvertently bucking the stronger gender stereotypes of the fifties. Like many another contrarian, I discovered the market had gone too far in its herd underestimation of the pink-collar commercial track. Its skills have paid generous dividends throughout my business career. You can retain a lot of extra information when you clock 85 words a minute in sten, and kids do not leave you behind during personal computer revolutions if you have never really needed a typist.

Not to mention that although the other guys made fun of me, I discreetly enjoyed being the only rooster in a chicken coop. The kidding was mild, since I had become a soccer jock of sorts, an ace halfback. Soccer has been a constant all my life, and during the three Bushwick High years, our team won every city trophy there was. We even beat out Cleveland High, which was mainly German immigrants. We were an immigrant team too, all but two of us fiercely competitive Lithuanians. The championship and ensuing citywide coverage earned the 'immigrants' the school's letter privilege and its respect: it was the first time in twelve years Bushwick had even qualified. It was grand to see my name in the school sports coverage, to belong, to be a winner for once. We even had a sizable following of cute girls over and above the cheerleaders.

Part of celebrity as a lettered school athlete is the pressure to maintain an optimal physique, so my ears pricked up one night when I saw a TV ad where a skinny kid at the beach got tired of bullies kicking sand in his face and girls laughing at him. He decided to take the Charles Atlas Bodybuilding Course. Within a frame or two the 98-pound weakling had become a musclebound superhero, chasing the bullies off the beach. I was sold. If I had chased Mario off before taking the course, might I not chase off his misguided older brother afterwards?

I signed up and spent hours doing the exercises, which I daresay had some effect. I was not quite ready for Marvel Comics but it certainly boosted my confidence. You needed all of that you could get, since gangs were rampant. They showed up punctually at school for their daily three o'clock appointment with idiocy.

A rumor circulated one week that the egregious Baldies were coming Friday. Their trademark was chopping off girls' hair and stabbing or clubbing any boys who interfered. We decided to teach these numskulls some manners. That Friday there was not a girl to be found in the school. Every boy carried a weapon, be it knife, chain, or bat. Some of the older guys even brought friends with zip guns. This was thrilling resolve and school spirit, but the Baldies never appeared. Their existence became a prime subject of theological enquiry.

One of my schoolmates was undoubtedly real: six feet and 225 pounds of pure muscle, serenely smug about his physique, a veritable bull, an utter moron. This time it may just have been my hypersensitized ego, but his arrogance seemed a challenge to spar with him too, on the sidewalk in front of the library. Using the advantages of speed and hidden strength, I quickly maneuvered him into a headlock, threw him and pinned him face down on the sidewalk until he cried uncle. The showdown had attracted the usual crowd, and when they burst out cheering it was suddenly clear: I was the scrawny kid in the Charles Atlas commercial. I had vanquished the towering beach bully.

These were the golden days when the junior "Blau Weiss Gottschee" team accepted me. We had more than our share of trophies and in 1955 I made the New York All Stars, which challenged a European team each year in Randell's Island Stadium. Did you know soccer was big enough in those days to draw 27000 New York fans? It was, but they were all Europeans; the only American spectators were the players' girlfriends. After the pregame field sports and relay races came 90 minutes of maximum engagement. The bench was crowded, so no one person got to spend more than fifteen minutes on the field of glory, but it was fifteen minutes of fame, the time of our lives.

The summer was packed with activities, so I had to start the day early to make sure I was back in time for my paper route. The boys knew they could not count on me beyond early afternoon, except on the rare occasions when I got someone to stand in for me. The subs were very reliable, but just in case, I would usually give my customers a week's notice that there might be slight irregularities.

One of these occasions was a Sunday when the Blau Weiss Gottschee team was playing at Lake Ronkonkoma, near Smithtown. Adi and I joined them, but not for the car ride; we wanted to use our bikes. 120 miles would be a cool workout. We made it to the lake, played soccer, and went rowing. Whereupon we realized we had picked up severe sunburns.

Were this situation to recur today I suppose we would hire a truck; there were still sixty miles left to bicycle home. But youth conquers all. We hopped back in the saddle and showed up on time, showered and dressed, for the Sunday dance at the Gottscheer Club House. Where does all that energy come from?

At sixteen pluck seems quite the same thing as manhood, and I had manfully pressed Edith's mother to let her come with me to Coney Island, swearing I would protect her with my life and have her back before midnight. She was reluctant, but she liked me and gave in. She and her husband were educated Gottscheers rather than farmers. Mr. Wolfe was a merchant and they spoke only High German, so some called them highfalutin, and their daughters did sometimes come off that way.

Our only Coney Island travel option was the Forest Avenue elevated train, with transfers to the subway and another el. This dragged out for an hour and a half, but I was beaming and would happily have gone all the way to London. On all our previous encounters Edith's presence had been diluted by her parents, or her sisters, the oldest of which played benevolent despot to the rest. This was a real date, and once we arrived we rushed through the rides and concessions to get to the real date turf, the boardwalk and the beach.

Claiming our spot close to the breaking waves, we spread out our blanket and started catching some rays. We were in perfect tune that day, both eager to share as much information as possible, story after story about our families, school, life in general. Now and then we took a break, wading into the waves to cool off, back to the blanket and the mind meld. My manners were on automatic high alert, fetching drinks in just the right cadence, scanning for sand-kicking bullies in need of the Charles Atlas treatment.

There was one terrible peril of worldly affection our priest had neglected to mention. When we went to go we realized each of us was lobster red, burned to a crisp in the fire of passion. But only on one side apiece. We had forgotten to turn the spit of sin. I was red left, she was red right. We were bookends. I was a dead man, a violator of chivalrous promises, a Bolshevik menace. Next stop, Siberia.

We reappeared at the Wolfes' door in excruciating pain, and you might say Mrs. Wolfe was rather upset. Ballistic. Edi tried to shoulder the blame, explaining it was not my fault, but the verdict was Guilty. Privileges suspended, parole date unknowable.

Depressing as this was, it got worse: there were still newspapers to deliver. Even a bath in water and vinegar could not soften the sting. There was nothing for it but to smear the burn with Vaseline and put my bike back to work. Every turn of the pedal was a fresh hell, the skin threatening to crack in a hundred places. That night the burn covered itself with walnut-sized blisters that took days to leak, dry out and peel away from the new pink skin beneath. Edith reported the same experience when I saw her a few days later under the thumb of her über-sister. I had to content myself with blind affirmations. All was not lost. Somehow redemption was possible if I bided enough time to invent a magical proof that I was trustworthy after all.

On the first Sunday in June Gottscheers gathered as always in Franklin Square, Long Island to celebrate the annual picnic with parades, dancing and reminiscing. They come from all over the world, from Canada, Cleveland, Austria, Germany, as far away as Australia. An entire cow is roasted and served with the traditional Gottscheer meats like Krainer sausage and smoked ham, and goodies like homemade cakes and pies. At the climax of the day, four finalists compete for the title of Miss Gottschee, with the honor of presiding over the year's events at the Gottscheer Club House.

We on the soccer team were popular, especially when we had just won one of our many city championships; but the popularity I craved was with the Wolfe sisters. One of my incessant crowd scans finally picked them up, clustered tightly behind one group, then another, aloof, virtually inaccessible, as if behind an invisible wall. Edi's eyes said she wanted to talk too but could not break away.

As autumn approached, my maternal Aunt Josephine invited me to her farm upstate in Saratoga Springs, near Lake George. Her branch of the family had already been here thirty years, and we had often heard of the paradise where they spent every summer, up from Flushing, where she had been a housewife and he a gasoline-pump installer before they retired.

It was dark when the four-hour Greyhound ride ended in Saratoga, but fortunately the taxi driver could decipher the runes of the rural address. A shack. All right, a cabin. The heat was relentless and you had to carry your own water from the forest spring. To cap it off, my maternal cousin Charles was already ensconced in the other attic guest bunk. Bathing meant letting the sun heat the water we hauled to our metal bathtub, out behind the woodshed next to the outhouse. Great, the American Dream was already headed full circle, back towards the camps.

This impression began dissipating when we discovered the car that had gone to its reward beside the barn. Charles and I had a ball driving it, one of us pushing and the other steering. We spent hours on safari in the woods: raspberries, woodchucks, Boys' Life generally. Aunt Josie shared the older generation's stern and bossy approach to teenagers, but she made some wonderful meals. Several times she and our uncle took us into town, to the historic Indian Village and the particularly educational old fort at Lake George. Much of my all-time favorite book, *The Last of the Mohicans*, turned out to have been set right around here.

The trip back to the bus depot provided the blessed opportunity to regain the Wolfes' favor. Nearby you could get in line for the naturally carbonated spring, where you only had to pay for the bottles. The next day the Wolfes accepted numerous quarts of spa water. A tentative pardon.

There was hope for me and Edi, but meanwhile the odd moments between soccer, newspapers and odd jobs would belong to the circle of clean-cut friends who traded cultural observations at the Irving Avenue candy store. The talent scouts at American Bandstand discovered our hangout and put the dancers among us on TV. Prudence counseled me to enjoy this one vicariously, being prone to trip over the light fantastic.

My parents vindicated their economic principles yet again when they rocked us in 1956 with the news that their fanatically saved pennies had turned into the down payment for a house on Palmetto Street, near Forest Avenue among the Gottscheers of Ridgewood. We would live in the top left railroad apartment, practically for free: once we invested in a hot water system the tenants in the other three apartments would carry much of the mortgage. I had saved enough for the boiler, and with Richie chipping in we had the house upgraded in no time. Wow, we had arrived.

Cleveland High was now the nearest school, but the prospect of transfer was drearier than ever with so many good friends in and around Bushwick, and both principals agreed there was no point uprooting me in my senior year. So I became a commuter, taking the Irving Avenue bus or the Forest Avenue elevated train, or just bringing my bike and riding directly to my paper route. My parents trusted me, so I often stayed late after work to study with Irving Avenue friends.

One night at twilight, as I pedaled homeward along Gates Avenue, I heard behind me the screeching tires of a convertible accelerating around a corner. Over my shoulder I saw it coming straight at me. Adrenaline sped me between two parked cars, jumping the curb and ducking down the Forest Avenue sidewalk. They circled and caught up at the Fairview movie theater, where six guys leaped out and cornered me.

Time for standard crash procedure: pull off garrison belt, wrap around right knuckle, prepare for mortal combat. Why on earth were they after me so specifically? They did not really know either. As they advanced one of them yelled "Hold it, he's not the one", and they turned like disarmed dream adversaries, jumped back in and screamed off on their quest for my mysterious doppelgänger.

The new environment and the embargo on Edi were subtly shifting my emotional course. The Russo twins, Robert and Gloria, were becoming my best friends. Their parents gave me high marks for helpfulness, though in truth my desire to help paint their apartment had a lot to do with the lure of hanging out with Gloria. Mrs. Russo also made mouth-watering Italian Hero sandwiches. I was with them when the call came that tore my world apart. Papa had been in a terrible accident.

It was almost ten years to the day since his miraculous return from Russia. Through Cousin Erwin, our Confirmation sponsor from Camp 5, he had landed a job at a Far Rockaway plant prefabricating steel beams for highrises and bridges. He had said it so often: "The safety precautions at this place are so bad. Somebody is going to get killed." And now he was the one standing between two piles of poorly stacked beams when one of them collapsed and crushed him from the waist down.

God had brought Papa back to us and now God was taking him away. God wanted me to stop at church to pray before hastening home, my head echoing with the unfathomability of the divine will. For this Papa had survived the war, the Siberian mines, the camps, the voyage, the unremitting frugality.

Richard already had his first car, so he took Mama and me to the Far Rockaway hospital. The emergency room doctor reluctantly admitted there was no hope. Papa would not last the night. He lay on his bed, both the sheet above him and the mattress beneath saturated with blood, the floor below a puddle.

Which somehow did not prevent him from opening smiling eyes and cracking a joke, forcing us to chuckle in the face of stupefying horror. "Rosa, I think you are going to have to cancel our reservation at the Gottscheer Club House for Saturday. I don't think we are going to make the dance."

The doctors asked us to leave them to their work. Not until the next morning was there news. Another miracle. He lived. Doctors from every corner of New York City had risen to the extreme challenge of this patient, this piteous mess, with his hip broken in four places, his grievous internal injuries including a crushed bladder, his legs fractured to pieces.

When they let us back into his room he was stable, flat on his back with both legs suspended on pulleys. While we gasped, he made a game out of working the pulleys to bend his knees, exposing the burst stitches on the kneecaps. Half the top specialists in the city had experimented with him, patching his organs, casting his legs, bandaging his body from head to toe. A gruesome pin at his hip anchored the silver bar running the length of one shattered leg.

There were still dozens of operations to endure before he could leave the hospital. Until the ordeal ended, Richard had to rush home every night from Trunz's meat processing plant in Brooklyn, where he worked with Karl, and drive Mama to the hospital. Sometimes I came along, and more than one day found me riding my bike down Myrtle Avenue to Woodhaven Boulevard, all the way into Cross Bay Boulevard, up to Rockaway.

Papa's disability check could not match his medical bills, and we risked foreclosure on the house, so Richard and I started paying room and board. Karl also found me a job setting pins for his bowling group, which met every Sunday at a Wyckoff Avenue bar with two bowling lanes in the basement. I would spend several hours first resetting whichever lane needed pins, then jumping back behind the wall that sheltered me as the balls knocked pins flying from both sides.

Afterwards the players chipped in for my tip, and as Karl had promised, it was never less than ten bucks. I pocketed it on my way out the door to soccer practice at the Club House. Mama was annoyed at me being away for so much of her weekend, particularly since soccer did not bring in any money, but I was doing my part and stood up for my one bit of regular fun.

Papa was never able to hold another serious job, but he did escape permanent disability and go to work cutting grass in a cemetery. He became the best grass-cutter they had, personifying to the end the family insistence on being the best at whatever job we took on.

I signed up for the "cooperative course", where the public highschools placed pairs of qualified seniors in real jobs all over the city. Each week one senior went to the job while the other returned to class, and at the end of the year the employer chose one of them for a permanent position. This was just the right incentive. When they assigned me to the copy department of the New York Central Railroad, at 460 Lexington Avenue in Manhattan, I applied myself until I could set type and work lithograph machines blindfolded.

Bushwick had begun revolving around the senior prom, with everyone angling for a date and rumors flying. The school paper asked who was going to the prom with Stalz and the other soccer champions. A good question. Edi was my choice, but this was taboo even assuming detente with her parents: she was barely sweet sixteen, while I was turning eighteen. Apart from her it was an embarrassment of riches. My peers might not have voted me Best Dressed, or Best Dancer, or even Most Studious, but when they pronounced me the male Most Likely To Succeed In Business they seemed to deal me the ace of hearts, propelling me to the top of the eligible bachelors' list. The yearbook shows a girl in my lap taking dictation. This was Jacqueline, not my date but my feminine counterpart as Most Likely, aiming for a career as a legal secretary; in those days girls thought success meant becoming a bookkeeper or personal assistant.

The girl who actually did me the honor was Ruth, a lovely Lithuanian with long hair and bright blue eyes. She started right in with my remedial dancing lessons, spending hours at our house playing records and drilling steps into my head until, to my astonishment, she could count on a half-decent foxtrot, lindy, rumba, mambo and cha-cha.

On prom night I was all decked out in my rented tuxedo, but since I could not afford a limo, Richie chauffeured us to the New Yorker Hotel in his Chrysler. At Wyckoff and Gates we picked up Ruth and I proudly pinned her corsage to her stunning white gown in the time-honored fashion. What a couple we made. At the dance, Ruth and her girlfriends were immortalized in a New York Mirror interview. We danced until we could dance no more, then piled into a cab with another couple for a dinner show at a Brooklyn nightclub, featuring one of the brightest stars of the period, the singer Vic Damone. Arriving at her apartment building in the wee hours of the morning, I escorted her upstairs to her door. When she thanked me and gave me a big kiss, it was heaven. Life was good.

It was practically the last time I would ever see her. Graduation drew nigh, and I was frantic preparing for my academic exams while working every other week at the New York Central. The blur of pressure was prelude to the cheers of my parents on graduation day, bursting with pride as their son received the diploma that made him the first member of our family to graduate from high-school.

America had fulfilled a great promise to me; it was my turn to repay its welcome, fulfill the vow I had made the day I set foot on American soil. On my eighteenth birthday I became eligible for the draft and reported to the United States Draft Board in Brooklyn. The law provided for random callup between the ages of 18 and 26, but there was no point in waiting. Getting it done now would satisfy me emotionally and leave me free to pursue my career singlemindedly. I was ready to serve my country immediately and asked the recruiter to "push my draft".

After graduation the New York Central announced I had won their permanent position, and I reported immediately. I was the office mail boy, with my very own desk in the accounting department, receiving, sorting, delivering and picking up all the mail for the eleventh floor. There was even a chance to use my typing. This was a foretaste of success as I had envisioned it. The ladder was high but the rungs were clearly marked. I was on my way to the top.

This new feeling came to the abrupt end I had requested when my draft notice arrived in mid-August, 1957. "Greetings. You have been ordered to report to Whitehall Street, to be inducted into the United States Army." D-day was September 15.

Saying my goodbyes was bittersweet, but my plan was working. My colleagues affectionately complimented me on it as they congratulated me on my induction and wished me well. By law the Central would have to rehire me after my stint in the Army, at an equivalent level of responsibility, and with two years of accrued benefits.

US Army, here comes the Stalz.

15

American Fighting Man

Private First Class Edwin Stalzer

American Fighting Man

The Induction Center on Whitehall Street was swarming with hundreds of bright-eyed young inductees and volunteers. Presently they rounded us up for instructions. There were forms to fill out, lines to stand in for our physicals and shots. Some failed and were unceremoniously dismissed.

A brief speech from a commissioned officer introduced us to the velvet glove and the iron fist. Velvet: noncitizens were not required to take the oath. Iron: refusal was grounds for deportation. I stepped forward that much faster.

After the swearing-in ceremony they ushered us into buses for the trip to Fort Dix, New Jersey. Having spent hours automatically following orders, we could finally look around and get acquainted with our fellow draftees. Many were older, reluctant warriors: the Army had nabbed them just short of their 26th birthday, when the law would have let them off the hook. My age group was a more typical and more engaging mix of two-year draft volunteers and four-year enlisted men, each with his own tale, be it sports or weapons or hot rods or girlfriends left behind.

Everyone has a twin somewhere in this world, and I met mine on that bus. His name was Siegfried and he had a revelation for me. This was the mystery doppel-gänger the gang had been looking for the day they almost beat me up in front of the movie theater in Ridgewood; he had clobbered some of them in a rumble and they were out for revenge. As fate would have it, Siegfried was Gottscheer too, and not just a Ridgewood neighbor but the son of people my parents knew in the old country. We became instant friends.

Two hours of New Jersey Turnpike brought us through the main gate at Fort Dix. The rows and rows of barracks would almost have taken me back to Austrian days gone by, had the fun not begun immediately courtesy of three DIs, drill instructors, who had apparently never heard it is rude to shout. They blitzed us incessantly with shock and awe instructions. "Line up in twos, stop talking, listen up." "From now on, everywhere you go, you run. Don't let us catch you walking." "Follow me, one, two, one two, on the double."

The march to our barracks ended in a scramble for bunks. Siegfried chose the one above mine; we were already inseparable. Our quarters proved rather luxurious by comparison with the memories they evoked: insulated walls, inside plumbing, showers, toilets, heat, even clean sheets and blankets.

Scarcely had we deposited our belongings when yet another DI appeared. "Fall out!" and we were off for our second run of the day. Orientation laid down the law. Our identity was about to be submerged in a set of rules, regulations and routines. Eight weeks of intensive training would turn us into lean, mean fighting machines. They would make infantry soldiers of us.

New recruits take time to forget the absurdity of the shouting designed to intimidate them into the reflex of instantaneous obedience. The DI role presents a ludicrous contrast between mechanical virility and organismic reality, and our DIs seemed all the more cartoonish since every one of them was obviously aping the sharp Jack Webb lead character from the recent hit movie "DI", even parroting his line: "OK, men, remember, your a—is grass and I'm the lawn mower." "Now when I say 'fall in', I wanna see a cloud of dust. When the dust settles, I wanna see a line of tall standing corn. Did you hear me?"—"Yes, Sir"—"I didn't hear you."—"Yes, Sir"—"I still didn't hear you"—"Yes, Sir", "Yes, Sir", louder and hoarser ad infinitum.

The next order of business was to make us look the part. We were already wearing Army fatigues but we had not yet been to the beauty parlor. This was the funniest scene. Grunts love popular music, and in 1957 everybody was an Elvis Presley fan, sporting long sideburns and long hair whipped into a "DA" (duck's a—). The barber was insensitive to these delicate masterworks of narcissism, running his electric cutter straight from the forehead to the nape of the neck, down past the wet spot behind the ears. Some of the sheep were not ready for the shearing. One smarta—from Brooklyn literally fought to preserve his prize Elvis imitation, and burst out crying when he beheld his beloved head smooth as a baby's bottom. The harder we laughed, the angrier he grew. The Army makes you or breaks you, and his tantrum was a prelude to a career of insubordination that finally landed him in the stockade.

DIs are the ultimate micromanagers, and during the first grueling fortnight of training the only respite from their omnipotence was time spent in line at the pay phone, but those of us who took it all seriously began to notice ourselves turning into real men. On the long-awaited day when visitors were finally allowed, Richie drove both my parents and Siegfried's, and they found the two of us posing together in our best dress green, our caps pulled down just above our eyes. We thought we already looked like real soldiers.

What we did have an uncanny resemblance to was one another. We were so similar that even our parents had to approach to within a few feet before they could tell us apart. Later, when Siegfried accidentally blew up a stove during field maneuvers, suffering some serious burns, someone came running past me yelling "Stalzer blew himself up!"

The testers decided that, whether half man or half boy, I was squadron leader material. The mostly older guys in my squad resented my youth until they realized I was not about to take advantage of my position: instead of playing the imperious manager, I pitched in beside them even on latrine duty. Infantrymen are not born the world's most devoted workers, but my men quickly grasped the simple beauty of the self-sufficiency formula I had discovered for chores at Camp 5: do everything fast and right the first time and you will have plenty of time off while the other squads are busy failing inspection after inspection.

The Army reprograms and professionalizes every detail of your existence, from making your bed to cleaning latrines to cooking your meals and stitching your wounds. You work twice as hard as a civilian for half the pay. Early on one of my enemies gave me twenty dollars to take over his kitchen police duties, KP, and I lived to regret it. Everyone hated KP: you spent two solid days washing dishes and peeling potatoes. My body took revenge by sending me to the hospital for ten days with pneumonia, and the missed classes forced me to play serious catchup afterwards; practically every moment was already booked for training and cleanup.

Green civilians do not become tough warriors by sleeping late. There was no telling when the DI would decide to haul us off to the range at 4 am. Our strategy was to steal extra sleep during evening time off.

Stalzer reasoning paid handsomely, leaving us the flagship squad in every phase of company life from target shooting and barbed-wire crawling to patrol and athletics, earning more than our share of "liberty" weekends for visits home.

Rifle marksmanship was priority one. An American grunt may sometimes forget his toothbrush, but his rifle is always clean. This takes relentless drilling until you can disassemble and reassemble M1 rifles and carbines blindfolded in one minute flat. Then comes close-range combat with fixed bayonets, and finally hand-grenade practice. You start with dummy grenades. After the order to assume throwing position, you hear "Pull pin, throw" and you have four seconds to unload the grenade. Then you learn to recover from a fumble: "pull pin, drop grenade, pick up and throw."

Dummies became live ammo. Each recruit had to pull the pin on a live grenade and hurl it over a thick concrete wall, ensuring the demise of an imaginary enemy. Everyone did fine until it came to Jose, an unlikely bungler given his tough Hispanic Bronx origins and knife-fighting expertise. After pulling the pin, he dropped the grenade. You should have seen us dive for cover as he adroitly picked it up and lobbed it across in plenty of time. "We were suppose to drop it, right, like in dummy practice?" We burst out laughing, more out of relief than at his mistake, but the DI was not happy. Dropping was only for emergencies. Don't drop it, get rid of it.

Being in tune with your weapon means little if you cannot hide and advance. Once you emerge from behind a tree an average enemy can nail you in four seconds if you cannot find fresh cover. Chance had it that our cover exercises came on a torrential day. When I spotted a tree stump less than four seconds away I fired my M1 and took a running dive. Spotting the deep puddle behind the stump, I made sure to land with my arms and legs on either side of it and my rear end in the air above. Awkward but dry, an elegant inelegance—until I felt an irresistible weight on my back: the foot of my DI, a black sergeant the size of a gorilla, forcing me into the shocking cold. He wanted to suggest a double combat emergency, not just submersion but also a sudden M1 cleaning disaster. Score one for the sergeant. His blaring face grinned broadly: "Keep going, keep going, the enemy is on that hill."

The next level was war games, the closest thing to actual war. One game had us in foxholes, crawling out towards the enemy that was firing live rounds only 18 inches off the ground. The enemy was a bank of machine guns, their vertical axis fixed so anyone below 18 inches would be guaranteed safe. Out we crawled on our stomachs, heads low to the ground, bullets and tracers whistling past, lighting up the evening darkness. Anti-personnel mines added dirt blasts to the machine-gun fire as we snaked past a row of sandbags to confront razor barbed wire. Onto our backs, using our M1 muzzles and stocks to prevent the wire from shredding our faces and torsos.

Half-pinned beneath the wire, we were ready for the coup de grace. "Gas!" A DI had thrown gas canisters into our midst. We had only nine seconds to disentangle our masks and get them on before the fumes hit. The adrenaline kept coursing long after we had struggled free and put some distance between us and the battle zone.

The game had achieved its objective. We had tasted real battle, the price of American freedom. We were soldiers. You can gauge the realism by the incident that forever changed Fort Dix training. One of the machine-gun bullets on this obstacle course was a short round: instead of igniting properly and whizzing past, it curved directly into a recruit's brain, killing him right there among us, prompting a permanent ban on live ammo.

Even before we had really regained our composure and caught our breath we once again heard "fall in". The DI shouted that we would be marching into a long tunnel-like building filled with tear gas. We were to take a deep breath as we entered, and hold it until the order came to strap on our masks.

As squad leader I had to get to the far end before the last man was in and the door shut. By the time I got there my eyes were on fire and my breath running out. When the order finally came, the mask went on as flawlessly as you would expect from a thousand drills, but a trace of gas remained inside it. You were supposed to use your last breath to expel this, but I had none left. Every molecule of that gas went deep into my lungs as I reflexively lunged for breath. An indescribable agony all the way down the respiratory tract. Uncontrollable coughing and gagging.

There was nothing for it but to run out of the tunnel into the fresh air, where I ripped off the mask and vomited violently. Boy, did I ever learn that lesson. It was hours before my breathing had any semblance of normality and days before the pain left my lungs and chest. Fortunately I was in the best shape of my life. Working and fighting more than sixteen hours a day had left me leaner and meaner than the Stalz who hit camp just a few weeks earlier, and well aware that bitter experience could prove a lifesaver down the road.

Guard duty was my introduction to more subtle aspects of command and control, though the first few minutes were simplicity itself: this was one of the many, sometimes random occasions where preliminary drilling from your commanding officer began with the the Infantry Man's Creed, the Code of Conduct mandating eternal resistance against surrender and collaboration: "I am an American Fighting Man. I serve in the forces which guard my country and our way of life. I am prepared to give my life in their defense...I will never forget that I am an American fighting man, responsible for my actions, and dedicated to the principles which made my country free."

Whenever memory failed you on any of the words, the DIs would jog it with as many pushups as necessary.

My job was to guard the ammunition dump, patrolling the perimeter with its ten-foot fence. The night was gloriously bright, the full moon casting shadows everywhere, the stars resplendent, the silence eerie. As always I took the assignment altogether seriously, even though we were permitted to use our live ammo only in emergencies. I held my M1 at port arms, out in front, the chamber locked open, the magazine ready for action.

About one hour into my tour, I heard shuffling in the underbrush and stopped to face it. "Who goes there?" No answer. "Who goes there? Identify yourself." Still no answer. My pulse raced and I released the safety on my weapon, slamming the first round into the chamber. On a night like this every creature within a mile could recognize the fateful sound of an M1 rifle snapping to attention.

A figure emerged from the woods. "Don't shoot, Stalzer, it's your command-ing officer, First Lieutenant Jacob".

"Come forward and identify yourself." The loaded weapon pointed squarely at the middle of his chest.

"I'm your commanding officer. Put down your weapon!"

"Step forward, sir, put your ID on the ground facing me, then step back five paces." The rifle was still poised to blow him away.

"Stalzer, I'll get you for this, threatening a commissioned officer". But he was complying, obviously getting even more scared than I was: here he was in the semiautomatic sights of a nervous kid.

He had no reason to fear a panic attack, but I was growing unsure. Obeying him would mean violating protocol and failing the test. Disobeying him meant violating the chain of command. On the hunch that a court martial would be more interested in protocol, I went through with the entire drill. He cursed me as I checked his ID and made him step back before lowering my weapon.

When he summoned me into the orderly room the next day I was sure the end was nigh. Instead he congratulated me. Most recruits would have cracked under pressure and received a reprimand, while I had earned consideration for the OCS, Officer Candidate School, at the Fort Bragg headquarters of the 82nd Airborne Division. A plum posting, and a trap, automatically extending my tour of duty by two years. "Sir, the private is greatly honored but the private is forced to decline, Sir."

The cherry on top of basic training was a twenty-mile forced march in full bat-tle gear. Not everyone made it. No one looked forward to repeating it. My squad assistant and I had to carry gear for one of our men who broke down in the heat and dust. This was the final step to becoming an American Grunt. You share your energy, your food, your water, your ammo, and if need be, your life and your death. You are no longer a boy but an American Fighting Man.

While enjoying our weekend passes we anxiously wondered what assignments awaited us upon our return. Most were headed for infantry divisions elsewhere in the US and the wide world, but a handful of us discovered we were in for another eight weeks of special training at Fort Dix. Some went to the motor pool as mechanics, others to the medics or the kitchen; for me it was the Adjutant Gen-eral's Administrative School, which taught everything you always wanted to know about running an infantry company. This sounded great, but proved to be a diploma mill for company clerks pushing routine paper.

The good news was that the five top students got their choice of assignment upon graduation. You simply had to study and outrank your peers, in a disciplined but businesslike, professional, almost civil environment. No screaming DIs. The highschool commercial track gave me a great advantage in typing, sten and bookkeeping, and my competitive instincts took me into the winners' circle.

Choosing an assignment was simple: head for Germany if possible, otherwise stay where I could keep the closest tabs on my future, Fort Hamilton in Brooklyn. In late January 1958 the coin landed German side up. After a short leave we were to report back for deployment to the First Replacement Battalion in Zweibrücken, a staging unit supplying replacement soldiers throughout the European theater. They would decide which infantry company needed me most inside Germany.

Not just my family but the entire Gottscheer community gave me something just short of a hero's welcome as I took the leave to put my affairs in order. Though still a private, I was a graduated infantry soldier of the United States Army, complete with unit citation, shoulder braid and a full complement of sharpshooting medals. Something the whole tribe could be proud of. Talk about feeling important: the entire Blau Weiss Gottschee team attended the boisterous sendoff party my friends threw at the Gottscheer Club.

Anxiety also welled up as it is wont to do before great departures. I would be away from home for the first time in my life, and for two whole years. Certainly great things awaited in the Army. Striving for excellence within a detailed regimen was a challenge ideally suited to my temperament: there was stability in having all the cards out on the table. But family is family, and friends are friends, and then there was the matter of that beautiful blonde girl who might not even really be here now, let alone when I got back. Still, how could she compete with the symbolic triumph of a return to German soil, a metamorphosis from refugee to American Soldier?

Edith accepted my invitation to join the family for the final ride to Fort Dix in Richie's 1954 Buick. It felt like I was going off to war. Though there was little time for goodbyes once we hit the base, I confessed my hope she would wait for me. She knew I was crazy about her and she promised she would write, but her ultimate feelings remained a mystery. Our relationship had always been one-sided that way, perhaps inevitably: she was two years younger, and while her strict parents tolerated my occasional visits, they had barely allowed her to date. Had it all been just my imagination, running away with me?

Grabbing my duffel bag, I vainly stifled my tears, holding my head high as I crossed the parking lot into the administration building, a man's man.

16

Land Ho

Men carrying duffel bags,
Bulging with
Close possessions,
Trod heavily up a gangplank
And then sail away.
It is with these men—
The men on foot,
The young men,
Where dwells the heart
Of America's strength
And security.

Boarding our troop transport for our trip to Bremerhaven, Germany

Land Ho

Fort Dix was swarming with units collecting new equipment and extra uniforms as they assembled for deployment all over the world. Those of us headed overseas had extra classes inculcating sensitivity for the culture and traditions of our host country. We were to be not conquering "Ugly Americans" but guests, earning the Germans' respect by learning their language and lifestyle. "Remember this and you will do great." Sadly, this intelligent approach was wasted on many of the young soldiers leaving home for the first time. Their idea of cultural intercourse was sowing their wild oats.

Deployment saw us loaded onto ten-ton trucks for delivery to the overwhelming Brooklyn Navy Yard dock, where destroyers and battleships reached as far as the eye could see. I had never grasped how enormous an aircraft carrier really was: a whole city block. Our transport ship, part of the same fleet that had brought us to America, looked like a canoe by comparison.

Bunks, narrow passageways, smelly dining rooms—all as familiar as yesterday, yet it seemed a century had passed rather than just six years. This time I was sailing not as a refugee but as a proud member of the United States Army. I would be pulling my weight, not cringing on deck with room service from Papa. Pride welled up within me and my heart soared on patriotic wings as hundreds of us marched onboard, single file, to the stirring strains of the military band.

Pride was not all that welled up within; it was time to renew old acquaintance with the wilted world of seasickness. The Atlantic is never smooth, but the winter months are the roughest, unyielding and unforgiving. Some merciful angel had assigned me guard duty. Cold and treacherous, but out in the fresh salt air rather than the sweltering staleness of the kitchen or the hold. To turbocharge the perennial remedy of saltines and gallons of Pepsi, and preserve me from even a single vomiting episode, there was another medicine: guarding the nurses from unauthorized visitors. Mellifluous female tongues can drown a remarkable range of sorrows.

The monster storm that swept in on our third day at sea had me clinging to the deck rail as I worked my post, for fear of being swept overboard. The gigantic waves lifted the bow almost violently enough to catapult us into the sea, then lurched us downward like a submarine about to dive, generating a wall of spray so monstrous that everyone was heartily relieved when the order came for all hands to go below, secure the hatches and wait out the storm.

The sickening ride in the cosmic amusement park kept right on going. My bunk was at the far end of the lowest hold, and every smashing wave vibrated the entire bow, sending me rolling. People went flying down the up stairs. Going to the head was hysterical: the toilets were lined up in an open row, and with every pitch of the ship a whole line of men would fly bolt upright, trousers around their ankles, and crash into the wall or plop back down as abruptly as puppets. We laughed our heads off, even though by this time no one but the core crew of sailors could escape the nausea. Not until the English Channel would there be truly tolerable seas.

Infantrymen are not infantrymen without solid ground beneath their feet, so it was salvation to feel it again upon disembarking in Bremerhaven after ten days at sea. The city could not be expected to hold the same novelty and mystery for me that it did for others, yet I stepped ashore with wonderment and great expectation. Three months before my nineteenth birthday, I was embarking on yet another great adventure.

The trip continued by rail. US Army trains also carried quite a few German civilians, and their predictability brought out the wise guy in me. The first thing any German said when he met an American was, "Do you speak German?" For years to come I would get a kick out of watching their jaws drop as I replied in flawless German: "How can you expect me to speak German so soon? I just got here."

Zweibrücken—"Two Bridges"—was a pleasant little city in the southern part of the Pfalz province, near the Saarland border. Patton's troops had swept through and leveled it during the war, but like so many German cities it had been rebuilt and modernized and now housed military units from several nations. There was a Canadian Air Force base right across the street from the Kreuzberg Kaserne, the headquarters of the US Army First Replacement Battalion, which also served the US Air Force. Next door were the German Armed Forces, and across town the French Army.

We were perfunctorily assigned to cold, square rooms in the Kaserne, each housing eight men. These were temporary quarters, the scene for a waiting game. Each day a few people trickled out to their final destination elsewhere in Germany. Except for minor chores, those left behind had little to do but hang around, eat, and sleep. The mood was too provisional, time too short to think of forming friendships. A perfectly sterile period, into which destiny slyly inserted the news that the Base Commander, Colonel Sam Wheeling, had just lost his interpreter and was desperate for a replacement.

In the peacetime Army a sane man does not volunteer for anything. This had been brought home to me early on by the DI who asked whether anyone knew how to drive. When five recruits eagerly raised their hands, he responded, "Good, here are five wheelbarrows. They all need drivers."

This opportunity was the exception. Someone with my background would be crazy not to check it out. I literally ran to headquarters and announced to the Sergeant Major at the front desk that I was fluent in German and wanted to apply for the job.

Thirty packed minutes later it was bye-bye, company clerk, hello Edwin Stalzer, interpreter to the base commander.

17

Wheeling's Marauders

Oberbürgermeister (Mayor) Roth, Major Martino, Interpreter Edwin Stalzer, and Lt Colonel Sam Wheeling on the occasion of Major Martino's retirement

Wheeling's Marauders

Colonel Sam Wheeling was no ordinary soldier; he had served under General Merrill in Burma during World War II. "Merrill's Marauders" were conceived by Franklin Roosevelt, Winston Churchill and other leaders at the Quebec Conference of August 1943, to spearhead the Chinese Army in a penetration mission behind Japanese lines in Burma, destroying communications and supply lines and generally playing havoc with enemy forces while reopening the Burma Road.

The saga of Merrill's Marauders was documented in books and the movie "A Dangerous and Hazardous Mission", starring Jeff Chandler. Lieutenant Sam Wheeling was one of the more than 2900 American volunteers who responded to the President's call. Officially they were the 5307th Composite Unit (Provisional). Between February and May 1944 they marched nearly 1000 miles, up the Ledo Road and across the outlying Himalayas into Burma, then fought their way through nearly impenetrable jungle, constantly outflanking the Japanese Army despite being outmanned as badly as ten to one. This was not without cost: of the 2900 men who set out, 2400 were lost to enemy bullets and tropical diseases. The Marauders received the Distinguished Unit Citation that July; later they were consolidated into the 475th Infantry, which became the 75th Infantry and spawned the 75th Ranger Regiment.

Colonel Wheeling returned from Burma with so many medals and ribbons that there was no more room on his chest. Perfect timing, since he was about to marry his highschool sweetheart, but the night before the wedding she was killed in an automobile accident. Sam drowned his sorrows in a bottle of Scotch, then another, and another, becoming the hopeless alcoholic I knew.

Translating announcements and speeches for Sam turned out far more amusing than translating dusty forms for someone else. As chairman of the local NATO Council and President of the German-American Friendship Club, Sam fostered good relations between the various military organizations, the local government and the civilians. Good relations meant good times. Once a year we even had a week-long competition between the Germans and Americans in sports like soccer, volleyball, track, and ping-pong. He had a special entertainment budget and I usually made up the guest list for the many great parties, which introduced me to the very best of the local Germans. He did not want his interpreter to have an enlisted-man image, so he sent me out shopping for local civilian clothes; at non-military functions I could pass for a German.

The work was often highly classified, so I needed secret clearance. The Army vetters went all the way back through my youth in Yugoslavia, the Austrian camps, American highschool. You can imagine the Ridgewood gossip when the FBI and CIA showed up, questioning family, friends and neighbors about my moral character, whether I had been in any trouble, as personal as it gets. They scared my parents witless. Some suspected a criminal investigation, but the truth came out in the end, and clearance was another feather in my cap, a real rarity in my age bracket.

Some older soldiers invited me to tag along with them and learn the ropes of the demimonde, so I started joining them on their rounds of the bars and hangouts catering to GI's, encountering the stereotypical cast of party girls and misfits. On one of these sociological field trips we were sitting at a corner table when a fight broke out across the room. Since it was none of our business, we went on enjoying ourselves until I felt a tap on my shoulder and turned around to meet a punch in the mouth, pulling us willy-nilly into the heat of the brawl. The sirens broke it up fast, but I was not yet in the clear, since as base interpreter I was obliged to accompany the investigating officer to town. When Captain Montgomery brought me back to the club I was sporting a fresh black eye, and when I went through the motions of asking the owner what had happened, he gave me a look that almost gave the game away, as if to say, "Why are you asking me when you were here yourself?"

Since I made it a rule always to buy the first round, I thought all worries were behind me when it came to paying my fair share; but one Sunday afternoon when we were shooting the breeze at another club, my buddies leaped up and vanished in unison, leaving me holding the bag on the last round. The bartender was not sympathetic to my plight as short-con mark; he barred the door and called the MPs. By the time they arrived to bust me, I had reasoned him out of his hasty decision: he had all my greenbacks, all my PX scrip, even my watch. The heat came down on my false friends.

The best dollar you ever earn is the one you are cheated out of. This was my wakeup call to stop letting a gang of idlers pull my string. Reverting to my Ridgewood status as gang of one, I crossed the tracks, sticking to strictly German establishments. Dozens of Germans, including the mayor and chief of police, were intrigued by so atypical a nineteen-year-old American, and they became friends, regularly inviting me home.

They also introduced me to respectable girls, creatures from a planet many of the soldiers had not visited. They were forever talking about women, but they seemed very hard pressed to tell the difference between a human female and an inflatable doll. No woman outside the pickup bars would have given them the time of day. Even inside the bars they were not libertines enough to beat the medical odds.

STDs were just part of the ugliness one could not but encounter within the first month at Zweibrücken. Racism too was alive and well. Quite a few of the soldiers were from the deep South, bringing with them their ancient prejudice against their black colleagues. The constant undertone of tension amounted to a sustained gang rumble. One night a Southern soldier ran from the shower room screaming in terror and pain. We hustled over and found him bathed in blood. Someone had slipped a double-edged razor blade into his soap; while he lathered up beneath the hot water he had not felt the sting until it was too late. Seeing so much of his own blood had sent him into a panic attack, scurrying off like a stuck pig.

Homosexuality was more hidden in those days, but we always knew one of the guys was gay. We tormented him with sly remarks, but his predilection never quite seemed real until I awoke from a deep sleep to find him groping me. For someone of my inclinations and religion this was a severe shock, and I must confess that I pounced and beat him almost senseless, to the great amusement of the other men.

Then there was alcohol. No matter what they tried to keep our unit alcoholic off the sauce, he always managed to show up drunk. Even court-martialed, stranded in a holding cell, he still managed to reemerge the next morning completely blotto: he had drunk Mennen aftershave, filtering it through a piece of white bread. They sent him home with no visible attempt at treatment.

No catalog of vice and misfortune could pretend to completeness without mentioning the root of all evil. Our unit was sensitive to its responsibilities in this area, with a constant round of card games, crap games, slot machines and just plain money bets. "I bet you" was meant literally as often as not, which was plenty often.

Despite all this we somehow found time for work. Colonel Wheeling's highest-profile responsibility as Post Commander was chairmanship of the local NATO council, consisting of the top officers from the American Army and Air Force, the German and French Armies, and the Canadian Air Force, as well as the local Mayor and Chief of Police. They met once a month to discuss local problems such as friction between troops and civilians, and regional problems including strategic wartime contingencies.

Colonel Wheeling sat at the head of the table; usually I sat to his left. He spoke English, which I translated into German, which a young German woman translated into French. His language was often quite colorful, but usually I could filter out the four-letter words: "The Colonel is not very happy with that idea." After the second stage of polite filtering, the answer would return in full diplomatic delicacy.

One day Sam was particularly agitated, cursing and waving his hands. When a string of obscenities received a response fit for Sunday School, he realized I was cushioning the blow: no one outside a Tibetan monastery could have absorbed so outrageous an insult with such complete equanimity. He exploded. "Stalzer, damn you, you SOB, what are you trying to do? From now on, damn you, when I curse, you curse. When I cry you cry, and when I laugh, you damn well better laugh." No need to translate that; everyone in the room knew it was me he was chewing out. I simply said, "I guess the Colonel is upset." The room roared with laughter and the crisis was defused.

When not in the euphemism business we were constantly dreaming up fun themes and guest lists for our German-American Friendship Club parties. I became an old hand at this; we had beautiful dances and ballet, and met the best of the locals. The fondest of these memories is of the biggest disaster, the Western evening with a square dance after the obligatory speeches and dinner. You do not know farce until you have tried calling a square dance in German. The vocabulary is all mutually interdependent, so when you try to explain which actions go with which calls, you end up doing incompetent pantomime while everyone gets hopelessly confused and the party melts down into a comedy orgy.

Lest you confuse the occupation of Germany with a holiday camp, I should remind you of our primary mission: running the First Replacement Battalion, including its annual field exercises, coordinated after extensive meetings with the Allies. During maneuvers the First Replacement Battalion both replenished troops and processed the POWs. I interrogated mock prisoners of war and negotiated fresh meat and vegetables from local farmers in exchange for cigarettes and other luxuries. My people usually ate better than the rest of the troops.

During maneuvers we survived on the bare minimum, as in actual war. Unheated tents meant wearing our warmest clothing inside our sleeping bags. The food on line outside was canned rations, unless my negotiations could provide supplements as they had in Camp 5. Sanitation was even more interesting than in refugee days: the latrines consisted of a hole in the ground covered by rows of wooden toilet seats where you philosophized with your fellow soldiers as you answered nature's call. Personal hygiene was a single helmet full of hot water every morning for a "whore's bath", a washcloth cleaning from top to bottom, plus a shave and a toothbrushing—try it for a few weeks sometime, if you want your home to feel like a palace afterwards. All these privations were for a mere support unit, with no fighting responsibilities beyond defending our base. The infantry had it much worse, digging frozen foxholes and playing war games.

A letter covertly circulating throughout the Seventh Army in the winter of 1958 announced a joke competition to "hunt down and kill" Elvis Presley, whose unit would be participating in the Seventh Army maneuvers. Everyone wanted to bag Elvis and the promised $250 bounty. The highlight of the war games came when a tank crew nailed his jeep with a blank at close range as he drove by around a bend in the road; it actually veered off into the ditch, spilling out everyone inside.

My Ridgewood friend Adi had enlisted by this time and turned out to be stationed in the same unit as Elvis. Later he told me that though even his tank crew could not resist the fun of the Elvis hunt, Elvis was well-beloved, a regular guy who shunned all special privileges, with only one controversial exception: dating the General's 16-year-old daughter. This he resolved in the end by taking Priscilla back to the States and marrying her as soon as she came of age.

Brussels hosted the 1958 World's Fair and my best Army friend Günther Scheffler invited me on a car trip there. To bankroll the journey we hoarded negotiable American cigarettes and food rations for weeks, filling the trunk of his 1952 Opel. We would survive on surplus Army rations from my connections in the mess hall.

Off we went through the Saarland and France. In Normandy we were awestruck by the fields of little white crosses for the thousands of young men who lost their lives in the D-Day invasion. Visiting the grave of my parachutist cousin was a very sobering moment Uncle John would be wanting to hear about.

Every corner of the town bore the marks and scars of the great battle, its local remnants enshrined in the "Nuts Museum". Uniforms, insignia, weapons, pictures, the works. At first glance the name seemed a wacky instance of the language barrier, but it had a pedigree: when the German Army surrounded the Americans and kept demanding surrender, the commanding general won the day by retorting "Nuts to you!" and ordering his soldiers to dig in and fight to the last man.

In Brussels the bed-and-breakfast operators had reps out on the street hustling rooms to tourists. Within half an hour we had negotiated with a cobbler's wife for rooms above their shop: a week's stay for four cartons of American cigarettes. The only downside was that we had to go up through the shop and past their apartment on the way to our room. We were convinced it was no coincidence that no matter what time we climbed the stairs the wife was prancing around matter-of-factly in her lace undies, smiling and wiggling her fanny at us. Heady stuff for young men, but not heady enough to forget the extensive knife collection we saw every time we passed her husband's workbench. He might not be entirely amused by her little joke.

Walking the beautiful historic streets, we heard behind us an odd voice calling out: "Me ami, Me ami!" Up around the corner was a man with a sandwich board proclaiming the virtues of the Miami Club. This we could understand. Surely there would be other Americans there.

Bad guess. The club was in a seedy neighborhood, the basement of a retail store, down a steep flight of stairs, through an archway to the right. We realized our mistake as soon as we paid the $2 admission and the door opened, crashing us into a wall of high-decibel music and crowd hysteria from the small, dimly lit smoke-filled room within. Realizing we had put ourselves in the market for trouble, I told Günther to stay cool as we walked the length of the room and took seats at a round table facing the only door.

Two females instantly materialized in our laps. "Hi, GI, you have American cigarettes?" We handed them our packs and each let us light one of the two or three they took. "You wish for us to sit in the corner?" Sure, why not. All eyes were on us as we followed them to a darker corner of the room.

"Here it comes," I whispered out of the corner of my mouth.

"You wish for us to drink some wine with you?"

We played dumb, though we knew perfectly well what she meant. "No, thank you." The reaction was not the chuckle I expected but an outraged shriek. One of them grabbed the corner of our tablecloth and gave it a quick yank, spilling our drinks and ashtrays, splashing broken glass in every direction. Before I knew it I had called her a most regrettable name.

Just two Americans in a room full of menacing Algerians, all convinced we had insulted their women, all blocking the path to the archway. Algerians were infamous for gutting their enemies with those curved knives. Some of them were even in uniform, presumably French Foreign Legion; who knows what blood-thirsty deeds were hidden behind their vow of silence?

We were not the dynamic duo. I was pretty muscular but only 5'10", while Günther was outright chubby and a mere 5'5". How were we going to get our sorry carcasses out of this one? My mind shifted straight into cold, calculating soldier mode, and I told him this would be the day that put our infantry training to the acid test. We would have to defend our lives. "Don't worry about being scared stiff, just follow my lead. We'll try to psych them out by acting tough until we get close to the exit."

Casually I ordered another round and we lit another cigarette as if settling back in. After finishing our drinks we calmly got up and sauntered toward the door, acting unaware that all eyes were on us. Shades of the big rumble at Willoughby.

Drawing toward the end of the room, we saw a mirror reflecting ten or twelve Algerians converging on us from behind. At the archway I gave the signal and we ran for our lives, up the stairs two at a time. To cloud the waters, I turned left and Günther right when we hit the street. They were seconds behind us, just enough to make them pause for the critical split second of indecision before they too split off in two directions, shouting and cursing, out for blood.

I could still swear we broke more than one speed record capitalizing on that thin lead. A perfect example of the psychiatrists' fight-or-flight syndrome. Flight hormones kept us alive to fight better odds another day, instead of becoming just another two anonymous "U.S. SOLDIERS KILLED IN BARROOM BRAWL".

Jubilation flooded our systems when we arrived safely at our room. We celebrated with a bottle of Gran Marnier, the whole bottle, on our panoramic terrace high above the city. When reality returned the next morning, highlighting the narrowness of our escape and the infinitude of a liqueur hangover, we vowed never to invite either predicament again.

For the rest of the week we were model soldiers attending the World's Fair as planned. Awesome, with pavilions showcasing the amazing technological breakthrough of the Sputnik and giving us vistas on so many different countries that we retraced the route home to Zweibrücken as changed men.

Back at the base, with the danger of our Belgian adventure safely behind us, we indulged in a few foolish minutes of strutting our stuff. Few were impressed; in fact, we seemed practically the only ones who had never heard how dumb and lucky you have to be to pick a fight in Brussels and walk away alive. All the world had long known Algerians and Americans were oil and water.—Now you tell me.

Playing the fool has its upside. Neither of us would ever visit a new country again without a complete briefing.

18

I Pledge Allegiance

I Pledge Allegiance to the Flag of the United States of America and to the Republic for which it Stands, One Nation Indivisible, with Liberty and Justice for All.

I Pledge Allegiance

A year had gone by in the Army. Before leaving I had filed my initial papers for American citizenship and they had issued me some books to study for the written and oral exams. I was already completely assimilated and saw myself as an American, wearing my patriotism on my sleeve and defending the American way of life against German skeptics. No one was going to disparage America in my presence.

One of my favorite games was to sit quietly in restaurants and bars where Germans, especially the older generation, were badmouthing the 'Ami'. On my way out I would walk past their table and drop a rebuttal bomb in perfect German. They were always taken completely by surprise, since to all appearances I was as German as they.

My long naturalization wait ended in late 1958 with a letter informing me I had qualified. This was so exciting that I asked the Colonel for leave to return home for the swearing-in. That he gladly obliged was no surprise: he had plans for me. Through his connections in the US Congress and Senate he had assured me a nomination for West Point. This was quite an honor, but it would mean committing to an Army career, and much as I liked my job in Germany, I was well aware the next rotation might send me to a completely different country where I would be not an interpreter but an Infantry Officer. I turned down the offer reluctantly, taking consolation in noticing that everyone seemed to think me worthy of becoming a commissioned officer.

What I was clear about was returning to school and earning my college degree once I got back to the States. Even in the camps I had shown talent as an accountant; perhaps I even had what it took to become an independent entrepreneur.

That winter I boarded the train from Zweibrücken to Bremerhaven again for my third Atlantic crossing by Army transport. Although I did not yet have my "sea legs" and volunteered for guard duty again to avoid the smelly interior, I was already somewhat inured to merciless, unyielding seas and fierce storms. Being on special leave, I could head straight home when we docked, bypassing base checkin.

On December 16, 1958, I reported to the Federal Court House in Brooklyn. The judge was well pleased with both my exams, saying "We can get this done in two days, in time to get you on the way back to your unit by New Year's."

"I very much appreciate that, Your Honor, but if it please the Court, since I am here I had hoped to spend Christmas with my family." Whereupon he very considerately wired Colonel Wheeling, requesting an extension of my leave on the grounds that such complex proceedings would surely take at least two weeks.

When Colonel Wheeling came through for me I had a bonus reason to be grateful: for Christmas Eve I had a special treat, a dinner invitation at the Wolfes'. A chance to see where I stood. Did I really have a girlfriend back in the States, or were they just being friendly again?

The walk to Middle Village from Ridgewood was a glorious three or four miles through a blizzard that had put the buses out of service, playing Saint Nikolaus with a bag full of small gifts for the entire family. For Edie I had a watch inscribed "to Edith, love Eddie". What a dreamer I was. After we enjoyed one another's company until midnight, making plans for her to see me off when I returned to Germany, things seemed to be looking up for sure.

My father meanwhile had determined I was finally mature enough to cope with the shocking truth about the birds and the bees. What a chaste man he must have been to imagine anyone could make it to age twenty in the Army without a clue; a world of trouble welcomed all who had not noticed a thing or two by that stage. Still I could not resist making him squirm a little as he beat around the world's leading bush: "Son, you know, there are, what I mean to say is, there are all kinds of bad women hanging around Army bases. You have to be careful. You know, well, there are some pretty bad, er, sicknesses you can pick up..." This cracked me up and I let him off the hook before he went scarlet.

My swearing-in was several days after Christmas in the Federal Courtroom in Brooklyn. There must have been more than a hundred people from all corners of the globe, all eager to take the oath of allegiance, yet I felt as if the ceremony were being held for me alone. I beamed as we recited the Pledge of Allegiance, followed by a loud rendition of the National Anthem. Not only was I a PFC in the American Army, I was now officially a citizen of the United States, a label I proudly display to this day. My sons, who were born here, find my enthusiasm somewhat exaggerated, but they would understand instantly if they had arrived on these shores as I did. While they were growing up they did at least get the message about proper respect for the flag: "I had to take a test for the privilege of becoming a citizen; what did you do?" I still stand at attention no matter where in the world I encounter the US flag. And don't let me catch anyone burning my flag; they would probably have to haul me off to jail for assault and battery.

The ever-reliable Richie was drafted yet again to chauffeur me back to Fort Dix for redeployment. Edith got her parental pass to come along, and we chatted about the way time rockets by. My tour of duty would end sometime in August, and as we parted, those eight months really did seem like the twinkling of an eye. Even my seasickness seemed less acute on the crossing that followed. But I would never be a sailor, and Edith would never be my wife.

19

Dear John

Reading my "Dear John" letter

Dear John

The first news upon my return to Germany was that my Brooklyn buddy Frank, the renowned dealmaker and smooth operator, had his discharge and was rotating back to the States. Waiting there for him would be the brand new Ford Thunderbird he had paid for by collecting cigarette coupons from nonsmokers, buying their carton rations at PX prices and selling them on the black market.

Knowing the scope of my contacts, he decided to hand the reins over to me. Mea culpa, the temptation was too great: just buy a trunkload of cigarettes, deliver them to a downtown bar and pocket the cash. The fly in the ointment was that you needed a criminal mindset.

Buying the goods was odd but essentially routine. Making the drop proved a different matter. Not that there was any real risk; I was a trusted interpreter to the base commander, coming and going freely at all hours of the day or night. But I could not find the off button on my conscience, and the magic lantern of guilt began spinning. As the MPs waved me off base it was glaringly obvious that they had already guessed the whole sordid tale of my descent into racketeering. My clean tour of duty had been frivolously soiled. I had shamefully abused their camaraderie, becoming an embarrassment to the base, a disappointment to my commanding officer. I would be courtmartialed and go to the stockade. The New York Times would demand a congressional probe.

As I drove through town every pedestrian stopped to contemplate my fall from grace. When I stopped in front of a store and a German policeman pulled up next to me saying "Good morning", he clearly meant "Assume the position, punk". Some even greater sinner must have caused him to drive off without handcuffing me, but by the time I arrived at the bar my nerves were so shattered that I just handed the bag to my contact—"Here, you'll have to get yourself another boy"—and walked away triple-quick, forgetting the money entirely.

Bidding the life of crime adieu and forfeiting the cost of the contraband did not protect me from receiving what was surely my "Dear John" letter from Edie. She confessed to a movie date with a guy from the office. She must have dumped me. They must have been dating regularly.

I was destroyed. I stopped writing her and never found out the truth, which for all I know was completely innocent and boring.

So far I had done no official dating at all, assuming it would be unfaithful to my girl in the USA. When I met girls from good families I pretended I was married with a wife in the States. One of the girls was a gorgeous little sixteen-year-old blonde photographic apprentice named Irmina Össwein. I had often chatted with her in the Rose Garden club, and watched her Rock-and-Roll club dancing on Sunday afternoons; they could do the Lindy like mad, flipping each other just like in the movies or on American Bandstand. Irmina called me "little brother" and I called her "little sister".

The "Dear John" letter freed me to date girls. These dates were far from serious, and one of them was nothing more than a dare. My friend Tom Fallon had been just months away from ordination as a Catholic priest when he suddenly went to the opposite extreme, dropping out of seminary, joining the Army and fancying himself a ladies' man. To hear him talk, every girl he dated was nuts about him. This grew tedious and one day during a pool game the devil got into me: I bet him twenty dollars that I too could get a date with Trudy, his consort du jour. He thought he would be taking candy from a baby.

That Saturday I saw Trudy at the swimming pool and we fell into conversation. One thing led to another and I asked her if she would like to join me at the Rose Garden for the dinner dance. When she explained she was supposed to meet Tom there, I talked her into blowing him off and going with me instead. For a twist, Tom asked to borrow one of my suits for the evening and I sheepishly obliged. Diabolical. You can picture his face when he walked into the club to find Trudy at my table. He stormed out in a rage and returned to base blind drunk at one o'clock that morning, ready to slit my throat, storming into our room and attacking me so viciously that the others had to pull him off me and put him to bed.

An old Gottscheer song says we have a tiny malicious streak, and this must have been it. Malicious fun usually has a lousy bottom line. I succeeded in teaching Tom his lesson, but at the cost of a friendship. Trudy was just a bet to me, but what if he really liked her beneath his bluster?

Even a raised eyebrow can have serious side effects when you are dealing with a guilty conscience. Some of us got passes to a religious retreat in Berchtesgaden, where Hitler had his famous Bavarian "Eagles' Nest" bunker high on a mountaintop. This was so far from base that we stopped in Kaiserslautern for the night. Not the place we expected to run into the Executive Officer of our own battalion. His wife was due in from the States the next month, and here he was, the rascal, with a young chick on his arm. Considering that we were on a religious expedition, the least we could do was remind him of the stakes, so we made sure he knew we had spotted him.

Later I found myself standing next to him in the latrine. "Hey there, Stalzer. So you're heading on a retreat. Need some extra money?"

I always carried what I needed. "No, Sir, I'm OK."

"Listen, you can always use a little extra." Ignoring my protests, he forced fifty dollars into my hand.

This was the end of the matter until payday, when I walked over to him and handed him his fifty dollars back. "Thanks for the loan, Sir." He turned white, then beet red. Only then did it dawn on me that he had spent the whole month imagining we were blackmailing him for cheating on his wife. Really we thought it none of our business; we had just wanted to make him think twice. He took the money and nothing more was ever said.

Sam Wheeling had two people with him at all times: myself and his Canadian-American driver, about my age. One day Sam told both of us to pack our bags for a week away. "Where are we going, Sir?"

"Never mind, you'll find out in due course." We drove to the Canadian Air Force base and discovered that the good colonel was trying to hitch a ride to French Morocco. As it turned out, there was no space available on the plane, so he instructed the driver to turn around and head for Saarbrücken. He still would not let on where we were heading, but after a few hours it became obvious it was Paris. He had been stationed there on his last tour of duty and still had dozens of friends there.

One of them, the widow of the former Ambassador to Belgium, lived right in the heart of the city and invited us all to the lavish party she was throwing Saturday night. She greeted us at her apartment door, stately, matronly, very formal, sophisticated in a long purple velvet dress. Looking over her shoulder we saw a lifesize portrait of the same lady, thirty years younger, in the same dress. Mrs. Price was living in the past. Her lavish apartment belonged in another era. There is something to be said for this; the party was so memorable that we talked about it for months. Sam was magnificent in his formal dark navy uniform with all his medals and ribbons. Not owning dinner jackets, we stood out like sore thumbs, but whether in deference to Sam or from noblesse oblige, the society types treated us like one of their own.

A name and address my mother had given me had floated around in my wallet ever since I came to Germany: a Gottscheer couple with a restaurant in Paris. It seemed too easy to be true, but they were listed in the phone book and welcomed us with open arms, even offering myself and my buddy a place to stay for the remainder of our visit. They were so delighted to see another Gottscheer, and a fellow refugee-camp survivor, that they could not do enough for us. I had to tell them all about Ridgewood and the doings of the Relief Organization.

The days that followed were a romp through Paris, climbing the Eiffel Tower, turning down streetwalkers, and generally being on the loose. Sam had friends who owned one of the biggest Paris magazines, and they invited us to marvel at their glorious apartment and sit at their bar with its hundreds of beer coasters from all over the world. They took us to a hilarious restaurant with completely medieval decor. The waiters were medieval monks and maidens, the walls decorated with murals of boisterous medieval feasts, the wine served in a glass urinal. To earn their cocktails, the ladies had to stand up with one leg across a chair while the headwaiter ran a garter up their thighs. Our frogs' legs came with a basket of phallus-shaped rolls; I will leave further comment on their production and consumption to the psychiatric historians of the period, and say only that their questionable taste added zest to a most memorable Parisian evening.

All this compliments of Colonel Sam Wheeling. Quite a guy. We could scarcely help regretting the return of normality the day after our return to Zweibrücken, changing "Sam" to "Colonel Wheeling, Sir."

20

Age of Consent

Irmina (Suzy) Oesswein, 1959

Age of Consent

For youthful naivete Romeo and Juliet had nothing on Irmina and me. That May she would be 17 and I a venerable 20. We ran into each other increasingly often now, intentionally, and each time our mutual admiration grew. Her friends in the rock and roll club called her "Suzy", and now I did too.

She must have been the loveliest girl I had ever met, her ponytail long and blonde, her smile carefree, her body lean and youthful, inspiring new extremes of fantasy and imagination. What had begun as mere flirtation became sincere affection, then love. Her spunkiness was particularly attractive, not just to me but to the other kids and her employers, Herr and Frau Roth, who had nothing but encouraging things to say about her.

Irmina had convinced herself I was a German civilian who worked at the American base and had a harmless quirk of playing the American. This suited me, since Herr Roth was a staunch anti-American, of the popular belief that only sluts dated GIs. Beliefs like this were not entirely incomprehensible; the "ugly American" was very much in evidence. Downtown you could spot them blocks away. The most notorious and belabored symbol of their arrogance toward the German way of life was the horde of American women who went to town with curlers in their hair; no German woman would be caught dead imposing her toilette on others. So Irmina told everyone she was dating a guy who worked for the Amis at the Kreuzberg Kaserne.

In retrospect, I may have been too much on the rebound, but I was hooked on this cute blonde girl and it seemed like I was falling in love. She said she too could not bear going a day without me. This critical mass of affection almost landed me in the stockade.

German-American Friendship Week was underway and I had to attend all the events with Sam Wheeling. That Saturday I spent interpreting the German announcements at a morning soccer game and afternoon track meets. At six o'clock Colonel Wheeling made a snap decision to officiate at the ping-pong tournament too. This landed me in a jam: Suzy had no phone and there was no other way to let her know I could no longer make our 7 o'clock rendezvous at the Rose Garden.

Sam was not interested. When I told him I had plans, he blew up. "I'm giving you a direct order! Get your ass up there! I'll see you at 1900 hours!"

"Go to hell", I responded as I walked off.

Multiple-personality theories may be a little flaky, but there is no denying the occasional incomprehensibility of our actions. I had just watched myself, me, Ed, disobey a direct order from the Base Commander. This was grounds for court-martial, a genuine world of grief. The whole date with Suzy was spent wincing at the inevitable consequences of my idiotic outburst.

At the start of a typical morning Colonel Wheeling would say, "Ed, come in here", and we would start in on the day's agenda. This time it was "Sergeant Major Schneider, get Specialist Stalzer into my office, now." So this was what my citations and my recent promotion had come to. I was about to be busted down to Private and spend four centuries in the stockade.

Sam was all business. "Do you realize the gravity of your action, Specialist Stalzer?"

"Yes, Sir", replied the woebegone Specialist.

He proceeded to lace into me with his trademark poetic language, working me over for a good half hour, painstakingly reviewing the concept of a court martial, the etymology of the word 'insubordination', and his estimate of stockade years per letter of the phrase "Go to hell". This man really knew how to put the fear of God into you. By the time he was done my self-image was a black hole. I was a featherbrained nitwit who had blown it all on a date with a cute little Fräulein.

When the mushroom cloud subsided he walked across the room and put his arm around me. "OK, Ed, got the picture?—What's on the schedule for today?"

No need to detail my relief at having shut up and bitten the bullet of his displeasure. Never again would I even dream of such a stunt, and he knew it. But this was not the last lesson I would learn about direct orders.

With my twentieth birthday fast approaching, I would soon be a short-timer, in my final ninety days of service. My short-timer calendar was already on the wall awaiting the moment I could begin X-ing out the days, and the thought of leaving Irmina behind in Germany grew ever more upsetting. We had something special, but all men are mortal and relationships tended to slip away. Planning to summon her from the States would be a long shot. If she was the one, this was the time to go for it.

On my birthday I took the plunge and proposed; she surprised me by accepting me only if we stayed in Germany. We discussed this for days on end, and I did spend several weeks pondering German job offers. The local newspaper wanted weekly stories for an English-language edition, and the director of an international construction company needed a translator for his business in English-speaking countries. Not bad, but the truth was that Germany was not an option. My calling was in America, getting a college education and going into business.

Irmina finally yielded, on condition we visit Germany every two years and return permanently if she could not get used to the USA. Now we had to convince her mother. Her father, a guard at the local prison, had been killed on the job several years earlier while riding between a tractor and its trailer, driven by one of the inmates. The tractor jackknifed and crushed him to death. Suspicious, but ruled an accident.

Ever since then her mother had been coping with a rather independent and headstrong teenager. Irmina's sister was old enough to be her mother, and her mother could have been her grandmother. Their relationship was constant war, and Irmina must have itched to escape.

A more experienced man might have seen a useful warning in the histrionics our announcement triggered. Irmina's mother stormed out of the house, sobbing, threatening to jump off the bridge. "So now you want to leave me, after everything I have done for you!" We spent an hour searching for her and did in fact find her on the bridge, whence we all returned only after considerable melodrama.

Later I found out she had often abused her daughter. Once, after gashing her side with a fireplace hook, she had locked her in the cold, damp cellar for the night. Irmina's revenge was to take a bite out of every apple stored down there. This was spunk. It was so attractive, felt so right, that a cynic would have spotted it right away as a likely source of marital woes down the road.

There was no practical way of getting married before I returned to the States in late August. Sam Wheeling had a solution: just reenlist and spend a few more years in Germany. This did not appeal, so he tried again and hit the spot. He would discharge me, assign me to a reserve unit in New York City, and after just one day, recall me to a year of active duty in Germany as a reservist. I would not even have to make the trip home.

This would give me an extra year to marry and buckle down, and make Irmina's departure less of a shock for her family. The perfect plan. I cut my own orders and Colonel Wheeling signed them. The reserve year which began 24 hours later was worth two years of normal active reserve, leaving me with just my six years of inactive reserve.

To fill spare time in the evenings I became the manager of the base Rod and Gun Club, opening, closing and serving drinks. The pinball and slot machines taught me why the word 'addiction' applies to gambling. Soldiers lined up every payday to play the slots, but the true long-term chance of winning was nil, since the machines were set to pay out only 45% of what went in, as per the Army manual. Some of these people played every cent they had. Then their wives played their allotment too. Once they were broke, they begged for loans, certain they were just about to hit the jackpot. Someone had to get the 45%, but usually it was someone who had quietly watched these types squander their pay filling the machine. He would walk up and hit the jackpot within a few tries.

During my tenure I commissioned a beautiful mural of a Bavarian scene, all along the back wall of the beer hall. In the foreground was a mountain cabin; a dirt road ran past it and wound up into the distant mountains, finally disappearing into the Alps. I loved this mural. When it was finished the Bavarian artist presented me with a miniature version, about 18" x 24", and it remains my favorite painting in our family room more than forty years later.

The Rod and Gun Club, strangely enough, offered not only gambling and liquor but also rods and guns. The guns were rentals that could only be used on the range, where fast-draw competition was the rage of the moment; we had all made our own leather holsters, beautifully engraved and personalized. The scoring combined speed of draw with accuracy in hitting the cardboard targets.

All supervised and quite safe. Then one evening one of the competitors, an Air Police weaponry expert, returned to the club with his Colt holstered. He drew it and started kidding around, twirling it before me in a parody of TV gunslingers. I reminded him his gun was supposed to be in his locker whenever he was in the club. "It's not loaded", he replied as it went off inches from my head. Luckily he was facing the window into the orchard; there were fifty people in the room and he would surely have killed one of them. This clown's recklessness infuriated me. I jumped him and belted him liberally until they pulled me off. Then I filed charges for assault, sending him to the stockade. One of those gun safety lessons you could not forget if you tried. "Unloaded" weapons have never looked the same since.

The deadly sin of envy had crept into the heart of one Lieutenant Roe, a field officer, who resented my role as sidekick to the base commander, maintaining I enjoyed far too many perks for an enlisted man. He was constantly looking for something to pin on me, and the club provided him with his pretext.

One night he called while I was tending bar and ordered me to the company office to replace the CQ, the Charge of Quarters, for the night. I politely pointed out that I could not just close down or leave the club unattended, and that finding a competent club standin on such short notice was impossible, though I did have a buddy I could recommend as CQ. This was too reasonable for a man who wanted my head. He responded with a direct order to drop everything. Great, he had forced me to disobey a direct order.

The next morning I was on report once again, facing Captain Monty, who was both company commander and base investigating officer. Lt. Roe presented his accusation and I my defense. Monty quickly ruled that I was effectively operating under previous direct orders from Colonel Wheeling himself not to leave the club. Technically I had disobeyed—he reminded me what disobedience could mean—but Lt. Roe was more at fault, having failed to ascertain my prior orders.

The petty fellow just did not have the pull to cause me the trouble that had terrified me when I knew I had truly disobeyed Colonel Wheeling. Several months later he was convicted of stealing money from the Officers' Club and was drummed out of the Army with a dishonorable discharge. It couldn't have happened to a nicer guy. He perfectly illustrated the saying my father loved: "He who digs a hole for someone else usually falls into it himself."

Major Martino, the base public relations officer, found a Polish refugee orphanage run by nuns, and our company took it upon itself to become its stewards. There is a special satisfaction in having the power to help someone out of a jam that once rendered you helpless, and these kids were much like refugees, though losing their parents made them even worse off. We spent many Sundays there, sponsoring cookouts and games and throwing parties for special occasions like First Communion, having as much fun as the kids.

My first car was teaching me the downside of automobile ownership. It was a 1949 Chevy with "fluid drive", a semiautomatic transmission, and it plagued me from day one. Batteries seemed to die as soon as they came in contact with it. I put in a new alternator and the battery died. Finally I gave up and resorted to guerrilla methods. The trick was always to park the car at the top of a hill. Then you could let it roll down until it was moving fast enough to start itself if you popped it into second gear.

As luck would have it there were plenty of hills in Zweibrücken. One of them was at a cemetery entrance about three blocks from Irmina's house. On the now innumerable occasions when I picked her up, she would stand at the bottom of the hill at the intersection in front of the police station. When the coast was clear, she would give the sign and I would start my Grand Prix, shooting through the intersection and starting the car. The system was perfect so long as we headed for the hilly part of town, and for several months this zany routine seemed perfectly natural. Then Günther Scheffler rotated back to the States and I bought his Opal Record, the most reliable car I have ever owned. We graduated from slapstick to travel documentary, spending many a happy day in the quaint villages and byways of Germany.

21

Chapel of Love

Ed and Irmina, when love was still in bloom

Chapel of Love

Irmina's sisters and their husbands took a liking to me and got us across the last hurdle, her mother's explicit blessing. There was just one thing we had overlooked: I was not yet twenty-one. I needed permission too.

My father was certain to give me a whole list of objections. What made me think I could support a wife? What exactly did I expect from a girl of seventeen? What was I thinking? In preparation for the showdown I kept rehearsing my list of counterpunches. How could I walk away from the girl I loved? How could I back out of true love, the chance of a lifetime?

To my shock, Papa said yes right away. Not one objection. I was incredulous, almost disappointed at being deprived of my chance to pack the imaginary courtroom and win over the judge with my lofty amorous rhetoric.

Many years later an obscure flash of intuition prompted me to ask him out of a clear blue sky: "Papa, were you surprised back in 1960 when Irmina came off the plane with a flat tummy?" He turned all shades of red. Aha. He had assumed I was doing the honorable thing after doing the dishonorable thing. He denied it, but I was on to him.

Swallowing the disappointment that none of my family would be able to attend the wedding, we pressed onward with preparations for the great day, November 12, 1959. There were wines to taste, a wedding gown to sew, a tuxedo to fit. "Hong Kong Charlie" took my measurements and eight weeks later I had my custom tuxedo; it still fits like a glove. Irmina's mother arranged kitchen help for the receptions—plural: since her house was too small for the whole guest list, we agreed to invite Irmina's circle on Saturday after the wedding and mine the next day.

Scheduling snafus created a one-week delay between the civil ceremony at City Hall and Holy Matrimony at the Catholic church, and the men ribbed me unmercifully about having to live on base for an extra monkish week, but the blissful blur of the event was worth it: the church bell summoning the town to the holy celebration, the priest receiving us at the church door and escorting us inside, my new brother-in-law Werner beside me as my best man. The organ filled the church with joyful music as we took our places at the altar and an astonishing number of guests filed in, Irmina's family and friends, Americans from the base, even people we had never met, Germans drawn by the tolling of the bell.

Then an unbelievable surprise. Adi, my best buddy from Ridgewood, came strolling in as if he had just sauntered over from around the corner. He was stationed in Augsburg, two hundred miles away, but he had made it to my wedding on time and it felt like family when he waved and gave me the 'V' sign for victory.

The congregation fell silent and the wedding march announced the appearance of Irmina, looking like a princess in her long white veiled gown, on the arm of my other brother-in-law, who was giving her away in lieu of a father. Panic seized me. Was this real? Was I really becoming a married man? Was I really about to make a commitment for life? Was I really ready to forsake all others?

Yes, yes, yes. This was a dream come true, just look at that radiant girl, every German boy in town was green with envy. Bring it on, Stalzer is ready.

The ceremony went off without a hitch. For better or for worse, in sickness and in health, for richer or for poorer, 'til death did us part. Werner produced the rings, the marital candles were lit, and as we said I Do, gazing deep into one another's eyes, we meant it from the bottom of our hearts. "I now pronounce you man and wife" rang in my ears like an angelic proclamation. "You may kiss the bride"—surely this was a movie. Lifting the veil and looking into the eyes of my wife was fulfillment, not unmixed with pride. A magic sensation of being the perfect couple, in exquisite raiments, at such an apex of felicity that it brought tears to many of the assembled faces, not least the German boys who had lost out to the magnetic Ami.

Off to the house for the first of the two receptions. The living room was decked out and tables set up in an L shape around two sides of the room, leaving ample room for dancing. Records played happy Viennese waltzes as course after delicious course of food streamed in from the kitchen, better than in a restaurant. Wine poured like water.

Somewhere in the whirl I had a chance to catch up with Adi and get the lowdown on his Army career. He had enlisted shortly after I joined the Army. After basic training he ended up in an Armored Division and was sent to Germany. This was where he had met Elvis and learned to love the regular guy beneath the megabucks hype. We pledged to get together again after the honeymoon and did eventually spend a few days together in Munich. We have remained friends through thick and thin, and we still visit him regularly at his home near his son in Burlington, Vermont.

At three the last of the revelers finally vanished and we could collapse into our bed in the small bedroom laid out for us. A chilling jolt. As custom demanded, someone had played a practical joke on us. We had kept ourselves awake long enough to search the room for traps, but it had not occurred to us that someone might have taken out the center layer of the mattress and replaced it with a big basin of ice-cold water. They had rearranged the sheets and added down covers, so we suspected nothing until the moment we landed in Antarctica. Our screams brought roaring laughter from outside the bedroom door. The victim rarely enjoys practical jokes, and this was no exception, but at least the dastardly deed was done and they would go home.

The next evening we were right back in our wedding garb, still the bridal couple at the reception for my American friends. The food and wine kept flowing, but the party broke up much earlier, giving us time finally to catch our breath and concentrate on our own lives.

Hangover would not be a problem; watching over an alcoholic commander liable to embarrass the United States Army had forced me to devise a method of remaining discreetly sober at parties. Sam always had cases of Scotch under his bed; sometimes he was already tired and emotional by the time I escorted him to parties. My trick was to have one or two Scotches on the rocks, then give the waiter the prearranged high sign for the switch to ginger ale on the rocks. It looked just like Scotch and I always stayed cool and sober, leaving everyone thinking I could drink like Socrates. When I was in a naughty mood I would increase their misery the morning after by making up stories about their drunken indiscretions. Blacking out was so common that no one ever doubted me.

Thankfully no one blacked out at the receptions, but while they were guzzling wine I was guzzling ginger ale, and everyone marveled how much Scotch Eddie could hold.

Our honeymoon reservations were at a hotel for American soldiers in Berchtesgaden, Bavaria, the beautiful mountain retreat where we religious fellows had been heading the day we encountered the adulterous Executive Officer. The drive would take us all day, so we started off very early. Hour after hour I smelled smoke, until I finally had the wit to stop at a gas station for advice. The Opel had always seemed as faithful as a Swiss clock. Had it perhaps just been biding its time so it could fall apart on my honeymoon?

The mechanic reported that I had been driving for hours with the emergency brake on. It was a miracle the car had not burst into flames. Embarrassing, but can you blame me for having other things on my mind that morning?

Late that afternoon we passed through Munich and soon arrived at the foothills. A somewhat icy road wound steeply up and around the mountain. We were awestruck when we reached the town, an infinitely picturesque alpine village with sublime mountain ranges in every direction, but having urgent business, we hastened to our hotel and checked in. It seemed forever before we could escape the winks and knowing smiles of the curious onlookers in the lobby—anyone could tell we were honeymooners—but escape we did, and that first night away from the family was glorious.

The next morning we pressed onwards and upwards towards the "Eagle's Nest". Another narrow, winding road, but this time the left shoulder was a wall of rock extending all the way up the mountain, while the right shoulder was thin air, a drop off a vertiginous cliff. Just the thought of being that close to the edge is hard on the nerves, and the occasional ice slicks did not help, but I was hugging the curves pretty closely until we hit a sharp incline and my wheels started to spin.

Since I would need momentum to clear the hump, I had to keep my foot on the gas pedal, but there was no traction. I was in second gear, but there was no traction. As I ran through the uselessly correct checklist we drifted closer and closer to the abyss. Irmina went hysterical, screaming "We're going to die, we're going to die, Oh my God, we're going over the cliff!" I kept my head, but its contents were curiously abstract. Surely God had not planned so senseless an end for us, just days after we married, just hours after showing us all that bliss. And what about all my plans? Surely this cannot be the end of them?

The answer came when the right wheel reached the gravel at the very edge, stealing just enough traction to pull us away and up the incline. During our brush with death there had been a lovely meadow just a few yards up the road. It looked up toward another enticing mountain retreat, but our appetite for climbing was sated. Not until we had taken a walk and some snapshots and plenty of time for discussion were we calm enough to climb into the spooky interior of the car and cautiously make our way back down, clinging to the inside lane.

Staring into the face of the Reaper and living to tell the tale had made us even more grateful to have one another, but once was enough; the rest of our stay was spent much closer to the center of town, where everything was within walking distance of our hotel. By the end of the week we were happy to return to Zweibrücken, stopping in Munich for a wonderful lunch and visiting a few other scenic towns along the way.

On a whim we decided to splurge and spend a night at the most luxurious hotel in Baden-Baden, a famous health resort. Pulling into the driveway, we were the only Opel in a sea of limos and luxury cars, but we went on in beneath the immense vault of the lobby ceiling. This might be way out of my league, but what the heck, we would do it once, we deserved it.

Guess again. They looked at me as if I were something the cat had dragged in from the alley. We might be dressed elegantly, but our car was a dead giveaway. Middle Class. Unaccustomed To Wealth.

But refugees and rich men have more in common than that. I decided to play a game and inquired about a room. They had three available, ranging from $1500 to $2000. Enough for the down payment on our house, if I even had that kind of money.

"May we inspect the rooms, please?" This put a dent in their self-assurance, and they spent thirty minutes showing us the rooms before we turned up our noses and walked away. Irmina had taken it all delightfully well, played along just as I would have hoped. We ended up shivering in a tiny room at a cheap hotel, The Stag, where the high spirits lasted all night.

We arrived home full of dreams, expectations and endless plans, two happy lovebirds who knew they were young but also knew they were utterly dedicated to one another, exceptionally mature and practical. Irmina would become a New York photographer; I would work full time at the New York Central Railroad while attending night school for a bachelor's degree in accounting. Within five years Irmina would be able to stop working and we would have two children. Foolproof. It might not be easy, but we had both signed on For Better or For Worse, hoping it would mostly be For Better. What could possibly go wrong?

22

The Newlywed Game

The Newlywed Game

Marriage means never having to live on base. We could find a place of our own in town, using my government housing allowance and Irmina's allotment, a percentage of my pay. In October she had finished her apprenticeship at the Roth Photo Studio and now worked there full-time. Her special gift for making the kids pose and smile and giggle made her their primary children's portrait photographer.

At first it seemed sensible to save money by living with my esteemed mother-in-law, but it was a bad compromise at best: the tension between her and Irmina never let up, and after a long day on the base, plus moonlighting at the Rod and Gun Club, I was coming home to a bedroom scarcely larger than a walk-in closet.

The solution was a rooming-house where we could have a small kitchen, bedroom and bathroom, furnished more than adequately for our remaining six months in Germany. There was just one annoying beauty mark: no shower. You had to climb a spiral staircase and insert special coins you bought from the landlord into a shower meter. A sort of car wash. If your coins ran out you got a sudden initiation into Nordic cold-water therapy, which was a shock at first but manageable.

Colonel Wheeling was once again offering to get me into West Point, swearing I would make a great career officer, but the more I mulled it over the less it resonated. West Point would have been far superior to what I could afford on my own, but my dream was to become a tycoon—a "business typhoon", I used to jest—and that meant business school.

The morning after I had brought Irmina to one of our parties, a call came from the Commanding General of the Seventh Army in Heidelberg, asking for Colonel Wheeling. "Yes, Sir, he is not in right now, Sir, but I'll relay your call to him and he will call you back as soon as he returns."

"Don't give me that crap, Stalzer," he barked," I know he's in bed, drunk as a skunk. My operative tell me you guys had another roaring party. Here is a direct order: you get his sorry a-s into a jeep and deliver him to me today, or consider yourself busted."

They all loved that "direct order" schtick, and I was not about to get into yet another controversy about direct orders, especially with a three-star general. "Yes Sir, right away, Sir." I packed up Colonel Sam Wheeling and had his driver bring us both to Heidelberg, convinced we would never meet again.

It was indeed our last goodbye, but a month later I received a letter from Sam, with a return address in the Pentagon. His war record had earned him some emergency favors in very high places, where it was felt his eighteen years of distinguished service entitled him to withdraw discreetly for a final two years behind a desk rather than lose his pension. A happy ending for a highly decorated, albeit drunken soldier.

I went through two more Commanding Officers during those last six months, showing each of them the political ropes in Zweibrücken. The first of them, Colonel James Monroe Jackson, had a background as intriguing as Sam's. As a young second lieutenant in World War II he had served as aide to General George Patton while his armor and infantry roared through France, Belgium, Luxembourg, Germany, Czechoslovakia and Austria, devastating and conquering everything that stood in its way.

When Patton advanced on Zweibrücken the mayor sent out a messenger to notify him that the German Army had retreated and the town was surrendering without a fight. Patton accepted and ordered his troops to march in, only to fall into a German trap: the Wehrmacht had dug in to defend the city.

Patton pulled his army back and called in the Air Force. Within hours Zweibrücken had been so completely leveled that they were still rebuilding sections during my tour.

Colonel Jackson adored General Patton and tried to emulate his every idiosyncrasy, showing up at maneuvers in riding gear, in boots and helmet, a swagger stick and two pearl-handled Colts at his side, driving ahead of the column on his new Harley, quoting his hero: "We shall attack and attack, until we are exhausted, and then we will attack again." Plenty entertaining, but no one took a fake Patton very seriously; after three months he was transferred to Fort Nowheresville.

His replacement, Colonel Wilson, was correct and proper in every way, a real poster boy, storming in to put us on notice that his Army was going to live by the book. When he issued orders that we were to wear shorts during the summer, we enlisted one of our own, a talented cartoonist, to campaign for us with posters of sad-sack soldiers, their testicles protruding from beneath their shorts: "Please don't embarrass us, Colonel."

His sense of humor was lively enough to rescind the orders, but not to replace Sam. The salt had lost its savor. I was just another soldier, hustling for the Colonel, ready to go home.

Trier Cathedral was displaying the original Robe of Jesus Christ for the final time as we planned Irmina's trip to America in that Spring of 1960. This was a once-in-a-lifetime spiritual opportunity we could not pass up. Previously there had been public viewings every ten years, with thousands of pilgrims flocking from all over the world, but the Robe was deteriorating so badly that the Church was withdrawing it altogether.

The whole city was a mob scene, people milling in to line up for the spectacle. Joining the ranks, we waited six hours for our turn. Cathedrals are my favorite landmarks—no matter when one appears, I always have time to stop the car and explore—and this one was magnificent, rivaling any I had seen including my favorite in Strasbourg.

Excitement filled us as we approached the Robe. How many people could claim to have enjoyed such a privilege? There it was, no more than six feet from us, behind glass, the Robe of Jesus Christ himself. Just a burlap garment, vulnerable even to flash bulbs, but it exuded spirituality. The prohibition on photographs did not matter; its image and aura saturated my mind and all its mysterious splendor hovers before my mind's eye.

Joining the US Army family meant a few new responsibilities for Irmina. She had to take part in drills of the complex wartime evacuation plan for Army dependents. While the men stayed behind to defend the base, trucks carried the women and children to Navy escape ships, traveling a long top-secret route known only to the military escorts. Perhaps living in tents and eating Army rations for a few days gave Irmina a taste of the refugee's life. She hated it. "Army wife" was from someone else's repertoire.

23

Chomping at the Bit

Specialist Edwin Stalzer at the end of his tour in Germany—1960

Chomping at the Bit

A medical exam was one of the endless formalities required for Irmina's departure, but horror of horrors, her cycle was late. We knew the doctor would confirm pregnancy and that would be the end of our five-year plan to prepay parenthood. The only option was to treat the scary news as a Stalzer stumbling block, turn it into a steppingstone. Somehow there had to be a way to accelerate my career and support a family.—Her period started in the doctor's waiting room. Close shave. We cleaned up our rhythm act.

Marriage to an American citizen made things easier for Irmina, but there was still no shortage of red tape, so I decided to see her safely off well in advance rather than risk her running into some fatal snag while I was stuck in the States, powerless to help. She would get a headstart on living with my parents in the Ridgewood railroad apartment; we had promised them it would only be until we had our own place.

The farewell was hard on Irmina, who was leaving her country, and family, and husband, at 18 to spend four months with in-laws she had never met. She flew out of Frankfurt into Idlewild, now Kennedy Airport, and Richie and his new German wife Irmgard brought my parents to meet her. The disorientation must have been overwhelming: first four new people looking her up and down, then a disappointing railroad flat to replace her modern German home. Letting her go alone was a terrible mistake, the first wind shear in 25 years of turbulent marriage. Though her initial letters were encouraging, I could feel I had let her down. Time dilated to an agonizing standstill, reminding me a million times that my wife was in New York while I was stuck in Zweibrücken.

Restlessness finally drove me to apply for a hardship early discharge. The Commander was not interested in helping me, since he needed my services, but my chaplain pushed it through, pouring balm on my inflamed heart. Instead of serving until mid-September I would be rotated back to Fort Dix and finally discharged in New Jersey.

Before I knew it I had broken in my successor, said my goodbyes and boarded the train out of Zweibrücken, this time memorizing the scenery, attending to every detail of the familiar route, knowing I would probably never travel it again. At Bremerhaven we boarded the USS General G.M. Randall, an undistinguished transport ferrying GIs back and forth across the Atlantic. Here too, on my fifth and final crossing, blessed with relatively calm seas, I walked every nook and cranny of the ship, trying to internalize all the cabins, crowded decks and bunks, even studying a booklet on the ship's interior and procedures.

What a difference thirty months had made. The green kid who arrived in Germany was now almost 21, more experienced than many men twice that age, rushing back into the arms of a beautiful young wife.

Hanging around waiting for my discharge proved no less excruciating in Fort Dix than it had been in Zweibrücken. Why was I still here when my wife had already been without me for two unhappy months? Impatience won out over good judgment. Clearly what I needed was a weekend off, proper permission or no. I went AWOL.

MPs were on constant lookout for stray GIs, demanding papers, and I had to dodge them on the bus to the Port Authority, even on the subway. Getting caught this time would have been the stupidest of endings, but I made it back to Ridgewood undetected.

The reunion was heavenly, but the living arrangements would clearly have to change as soon as I had work. They were deluxe for a refugee camp, but ridiculous given Irmina's background. My parents had thoughtfully given us the last and most private room, but that was not saying much: only a sliding wood curtain divided us from them, and we had to barge past to get to the bathroom. Try letting go with your wife when you can hear your parents breathing ten feet away; it will deepen your admiration for Marcel Marceau. No matter, within a few months we would be on our way and laughing.

No one at Fort Dix caught on; God must have winked.

24

American Dream Diary

Grand Central Station and 466 Lexington Avenue, New York City

American Dream Diary

The Army's farewell was an interminable series of debriefings to prepare us for the transition to civilian life. There were sessions on how to land the job I had already landed at the New York Central Railroad, and reassignments to Reserve organizations. Most boys would have monthly meetings and annual training camps; fortunately I was exempted from these, being a returning reservist with a year's active duty behind me, but for six more years I would remain attached to a New York City regiment of the inactive reserve, ready to be called up in a national emergency.

For months I had corresponded with my former employers at the New York Central, and after my discharge I wasted no time contacting them to take up the Accounting Clerk post they had waiting for me. They said to report the next Monday. Bingo, twin homecomings. I was reunited with my wife and gainfully employed.

The absence of change in the office was remarkable enough to make me half unsure I had ever really left. Many of my colleagues were still sitting in the same jobs, at the very same desks where they had wished me good luck on my Army tour. Before I knew it I was completely reacclimated.

The New York Central was a pioneer in electronic data processing, with large mainframes already crunching mountains of numbers, spitting out reams of reports. General-purpose processors had not yet come into their own; programming meant hand-wiring circuit boards, and a mainframe had less memory than the watch on my wrist today. But there was plenty to learn as I burst the reports and delivered the carbon copies to various offices.

Irmina was still endearingly naive, answering photographic job ads in Harlem and the Bowery, unconvinced when I insisted she turn down offers from such dangerous neighborhoods. Then luck presented an opening at Axel Grosser's Lexington Avenue photo lab. Axel was delighted to find someone with skills so rare in New York City, and we were delighted that he was German and the studio only blocks away from my office. Instead of worrying about Irmina being alone on the subway, I could commute with her and enjoy more of her rapid progress in the English language and the American Way; soon she could pass for a young American professional.

The opinionated willfulness that had attracted me to her in the first place was beginning to invite confrontations. We were both born under the sign of Taurus, and I too can be stern and bullheaded. When we locked horns, the sparks flew, but the reconciliations could be ecstatic. This seemed par for the course; how could two people be expected to agree on every single thing? Tempests were as natural in marriage as in the atmosphere. It did not occur to us that the atmospheres of some planets can boil into sulfuric-acid storms.

John F. Kennedy had just won the presidency when a labor dispute erupted between the New York Central and the Tugboat Union, which hauled perishables onto the docks and from there into railroad cars. Upper management informed us younger men that we had volunteered to work the docks as strikebreakers. Quite a few of us were veterans and as part of management we felt we had no choice but to obey the direct order of Al Pearlman, president of the company, who promised us all the extras we needed to fight the bitter cold: sturdy boots, heavy underwear, parkas, gloves, jackets, hats.

The conflict had been raging for a month when my bus arrived at the settlement of sleeping and dining cars set up to house and feed us while the longshoremen warmed themselves at dozens of fires in fifty-gallon drums outside. We were back in the Army. They told us mounted police would guarantee our safety, on strict condition we did not stray from the compound.

We crossed the picket lines every day, longshoremen menacing us as we passed, cargo hooks protruding from their waistbands. The police managed to hold them back but even their jeers were frightening. By the day Kennedy's inaugural speech came over the radio we felt we were living in an armed camp. Nonetheless we saved thousands of tons of perishable food, routinely coping with 75% of the regulars' workload.

Management was pleased, but our families were not. One day when Irmina and I were on the phone wishing we were together, I announced I could stand it no more and had a plan to sneak home for a few hours. She was frightened for my job, but I assured her I had been thinking it through and knew exactly the right hole in the wall. That night love sent me AWOL again, wading through waist-high snow, running to the subway. Two hours later I was home in Ridgewood. The next morning found me in my sleeping car when breakfast came, with no one the wiser. God had winked again, though this time He had me leave round-trip snow tracks it did not take a genius to decipher.

Not one additional penny was forthcoming when the strike ended a few days later and they escorted us back to the New York Central. We had to content ourselves with the reflection that these were rough times and one had to be glad for satisfied employers. They showed their gratitude soon enough, with an opportunity for advancement in the Engineering Accounting Department at $75 a week. This raise was so intoxicating that I told Irmina she would be able to stop working in a year or two, when I would reach the lofty goal of $100 and be well on my way to the Holy Grail of the "official payroll", where managers earned a stupendous $10000 a year and really lived the good life.

By giving me the chance to shine at systems and procedures, Engineering Accounting became my springboard up through the corporate ranks. Our mission was cost-benefit analysis on elimination of grade crossings. Proper accounting would mean millions in reimbursement from the cities we served. My break came when the Comptroller gave me the goahead to streamline our procedures into a manual that would ensure perfectly uniform accounting methods, eliminating duplication. The manual saved the Railroad a fortune and put me on the fast track.

CIA meanwhile was going off the rails. On April 17, 1961, after months of training, about 1300 Cuban exiles were dropped at the Bay of Pigs on the southeast coast of Cuba. The revelation of Kennedy's involvement in the disastrous invasion embarrassed his Administration so seriously that we in the inactive reserve had reason to worry we would be returned to active duty, but fortunately our careers were not to be so rudely interrupted.

That spring I discovered I already had sufficient credits to enroll at Pace College. The only obstacle was the requirement that I catch up in advanced algebra during the first semester; but there is a book for everything, and "Advanced Algebra for Beginners" was just what the doctor ordered. After studying and cramming, algebra was still Greek to me, but I had memorized enough formulas to pass with a B.

Pace was too expensive, so after the first year of night school I transferred to Baruch Business College, a division of New York City College. Six years of night school and several jobs later I would graduate with a Bachelor of Business Administration in accounting, eventually proceeding to a two-year correspondence course in Business Law with the LaSalle Institute in Chicago, and finally a two-year course with the Alexander Hamilton Institute, receiving the equivalent of an MBA.

During 1962 this meant night school as many as four times a week. The merry-go-round started with 5am studies for the evening ahead, and an extra study hour on the train to Manhattan. The first class after a full workday was at six o'clock, and sometimes I did not make it home until midnight. The strange thing was how normal it all felt.

Given my hard-earned reputation as ready, willing and able to take on any challenge thrown at me, I was the natural candidate when the Disbursement Department lost its venerable disbursement analyst. Very well, but what was a disbursement analyst? No one knew. He had spent forty years on the job without anyone venturing to ask. Would I get a raise? Yes, but I would have to train myself. Fair enough, there are plenty worse things than being your own judge and jury.

The mystery man turned out to have authored decades of reports on the dining-car and sleeping-car operations. Copies were readily available and the format could be mastered in short order.

To put my best foot forward I decided to deliver the first batch in person to the Vice President's office on Park Avenue. The secretary thanked me, but rather than leave them in his box she sorted them directly into her orderly file cabinet. When I asked her why, she said this was what she had been taught to do with them when she arrived fifteen years earlier. So when were they picked up? Never, really. Twenty years ago the Vice President had inspected one, but since then, my predecessor had ritually delivered and the secretary had ceremonially filed. In fact his pristine obscurity had survived three different Vice Presidents with four different secretaries.

Checking the rest of the distribution list in person, I discovered 75% of the job could be eliminated. This man had gone his rounds through the Twilight Zone for forty years and retired with a generous pension. Is it any wonder the New York Central eventually went bankrupt?

Instead of putting myself out of a job I received yet another promotion, a commission on all the money saved. I was the department's "efficiency expert", the scourge of economic zombies, traveling throughout the system on my special pass, establishing standards through time-and-motion studies on methods and procedures, then writing up procedural manuals. Meanwhile night school was opening up new and powerful disciplines and my wary eye eventually spotted an opportunity for advancement through the Tax Department, where I was to stay until another company offered me even better pay.

National emergency remained the subtext of the early sixties, and on October 17, 1962 the Cuban Missile Crisis erupted to rock my life. The Soviets were installing medium-range nuclear missiles in Cuba, prompting President Kennedy to blockade their ships. This time our unit went on red alert, ready for war. At a moment's notice we could go active. This personalized the already gripping emotion of the next two weeks, as the confrontation between Kruschev and Kennedy brought the world to the brink of nuclear war.

Even at such moments the minor irritants of domestic life continue their Chinese water torture. Living under my parents' constant scrutiny was no picnic. We escaped when one of the downstairs apartments went vacant and my parents moved into it. Having our own apartment was blessed relief, and we remodeled from top to bottom: new kitchen, new bath, new carpets, paint, wallpaper, furniture.

Who will ever forget where they were or what they were doing at 1:40 pm on November 22, 1963, when Walter Cronkite announced that shots had been fired at the President's motorcade in downtown Dallas, that it appeared the President was hit? The whole world stopped in its tracks, unsure how severe the damage might be. I was on my way back from lunch when I heard the gasps of disbelief from the crowd assembling around the television in the main terminal of Grand Central Station.

Television mesmerized every corner of the civilized world as events unfolded over the next four days. The President was indeed dead. Lyndon Johnson took the oath of office on Air Force One, with Jacqueline Kennedy standing beside him in a bloodstained dress. The nation cried along as the mourners accompanied the caissons transferring the coffin from the Capitol Rotunda to St. Matthew's Cathedral for the solemn funeral mass, then across the Potomac to Arlington National Cemetery. History will never forget the image of the three-year-old John F. Kennedy, Jr. saluting at the lowering of the casket.

This was to be the year I met my first mentor. Leo Kaiser was president of an apparel company in mid-Manhattan. His wife Margot was an amateur photographer who brought her film to Irmina's lab, where they became friends. One night Leo and I arrived there simultaneously to pick up our wives. One thing led to another and Leo asked me whether I would be interested in coming to work for him. "I could use a young man like you."

The mouth of the gift horse did not look too kissable at first to a young Stalzer who thought he was on the fast track at the New York Central, but Leo badgered me until he persuaded me to visit his office on the 34th Floor of the Sperry Rand Building on Sixth Avenue. Rockefeller Center would be right out my office window, not a bad perk, but Leo opened my eyes to the more important implications. Small companies offered more openings for rapid advancement. Within a few weeks I was completely sold, signing on as Controller and Credit Manager, big-league accounting at a salary approaching the Railroad's "official payroll".

Like most people I would end up working for, Leo was a go-getter, a brilliant businessman who had lifted himself by his bootstraps from salesman to company president. He had just been promoted into the top slot when we met. During our years together we acquired another company and were acquired in turn, joining the other 36 divisions of the Kaiser Roth Corporation with its yearly turnover of $600 million. I soon had the additional title Assistant to the President and was involved in every aspect of the business, an avid disciple of Leo and, by the time I left, an accomplished entrepreneur in my own right.

Leo's precept "Your first loss is your best loss" has held up through forty years of changing fashions. Don't hold on to losing ventures. Cut your losses, walk away and invest in a success. Never indulge in regrets if you did your best.

Entrepreneur Magazine became my fountainhead of contemporary business wisdom. I read, marked and inwardly digested every line of every article, including the "Entrepreneur's Creed" which has remained in my wallet ever since, the magic formula for metamorphosing stumbling blocks:

> **People have a fuzzy concept of what entrepreneurialism is all about, but what it comes down to is: you've got to be willing to hang on a cliff 100 times, 200 times...be able to get knocked off and climb back up, I mean, it's hard. And the hard part is just not giving up. Your idea can be great, but if you don't have that deep well to draw from—or if you're not very, very lucky quick—you're just not going to make it.**

In essence: the difference between a successful person and a failure is that the success found the determination and strength to pick himself up after every disaster, while the failure stayed down for the count.

Just after I added a Dun and Bradstreet course in Financial Analysis to my virtual arsenal, the specter of physical arsenals reared its head again with the false but earthshaking report of North Vietnamese torpedo boats sinking the USS Maddox in the Gulf of Tonkin. Thus began the overt phase of the Vietnam War, with its 65000 American and seven-figure Southeast Asian casualties by the bitter end in April, 1975. As if some gremlin were determined to interfere with my move into the fast lane and the birth of our first child, I was back on Ready Alert with two years of possible active duty remaining.

We watched with the rest of mankind as our country plunged deeper and deeper into a war with no visible logical conclusion. The draft was revived for the first time, and there were ugly antiwar clashes all over the country, with a quarter of a million people marching on the Pentagon in November 1969 and more than 100 colleges closed by student riots climaxing in the killing of four demonstrators at Kent State University in Ohio. Throughout the unrest we cleaved to our belief in the American Way, the Flag and the Constitution, even as we pondered the purpose of the war. For us it was torment to hear about young servicemen returning to a divided country, bereft of honor. The Wall at the Vietnam Veterans'

Memorial in Washington immortalizes the saga of courage and dedication tragically abused.

25

The Gathering Storm

Irmina and Ed with Steven in 1964

The Gathering Storm

Well-laid plans take time to ripen into irony. We were right on track, five years into marriage and determined to beat the divorce statistics, when our first son arrived in October 1964. I was still a traditionalist, married for life, "for better or for worse, for richer or for poorer, in sickness and in health"; Lord knows we had seen them all and were thankful the ups outweighed the downs. But it remained a struggle, emotionally if not financially. We were maturing along different vectors, both far from our original intersection.

For $3400 in cash we bought our first brand-new car, a brilliant white Buick Skylark with a six-cylinder V engine, a black vinyl roof and black vinyl bucket seats, and heavy chrome spinners on the four whitewall tires. How proud we were driving this dream out of Manhattan, across the 59th Street Bridge into Long Island City, along Queens Boulevard to Woodhaven Boulevard, down Myrtle Avenue, all the way to Forest and Palmetto. A dozen people appeared to inspect it when we arrived at my parents' house.

This was to become my favorite car ever; I kept it in mint condition for 17 years. I would gladly have done the same with my marriage, but we were wasting more and more energy on trivial disputes, clear symptoms of deeper divergence. Irmina thought my career gain had been her loss: New York might be perfect for my ambitions, but she could have gone much further by now in Germany. What if she were to buy her own photo studio, with me as her manager and rep? No way. I instinctively recoiled at renouncing my inside track before reaching the top, and our personal tensions boded ill for professional collaboration, particularly if she insisted on appointing herself boss rather than partner.

Dissonance over the naming of our son highlighted our very different views about "forsaking all others". She had never hesitated to dwell on the virtues of her many male friends, her bosses in Germany and New York, her photographer acquaintances. Men do not like this any better than women like their husbands studying other women, so asking to name our son after her colleague David was guaranteed to annoy me, all the more so since I actually like the name David. Resentment prompted me to urge the name Steven and compromise on Steven David.

Parenthood suited us both and smoothed the waters. Fathers will understand my joy and pride at the birth, gaily informing strangers of the world's tenth wonder—"I have a son!"—and passing out a hundred cigars. Irmina missed her work and customers, but she excelled as a stay-at-home mom, reading every available book on her new profession, including our daily rescuer Dr. Spock. Steven must have had the largest photographic portfolio in the city. We had found a catalyst for renewed commitment. Our 'product' was a handsome devil, as might have been expected from his beautiful mother and reasonably handsome father. Blonde hair, the brightest blue eyes, a cherubic disposition. Turbulence approached nil; I kept my promise as provider and she as homemaker.

The next milestone came in 1966 when our savings became the down payment on our first house in Rego Park, a beautiful brick townhouse with three bedrooms and two baths, a lovely kitchen, dining room and living room. The walk-in basement was furnished, the backyard beautifully landscaped and surrounded by a 6-foot wooden fence, giving us nearly infinite privacy by Camp 5 standards. With Steven playing safely in the backyard, and the basement open for lawn parties and routine socializing, the upstairs practically kept itself neat. We could barely afford the payments, but I was as sure of a raise the following year as I was of capital gains on the house.

Traditional Gottscheer wisdom was to have tenants pay the mortgage on a multiple-unit house, so my parents did not understand us. Our situation was far from traditional; for a start, I was close to a college degree. To our minds, freedom from tenant hassles was an economic good well worth the extra monthly expense, which raises would cover anyway.

As if to prove us right, fate sent us another Gottscheer who had pioneered a new way of life. Right after we closed on the house, our closing attorney Joe Mitschel approached me with a job offer from one of his clients, a lifelong friend who needed someone of my caliber to head up the Fiscal and Financial Department of her Ridgewood knitting mill.

Another gift horse with bad teeth. What would a dynamic young man with a secure and elegant future at a highly successful Manhattan company want with a knitting mill in Ridgewood? But like Leo before him, Joe insisted on kicking me upstairs in spite of myself. Surely I would at least do Anna Friedrich the courtesy of a visit?

When I met Anna at the Friedrich Knitting Mills I let her know up front that I was not in the job market, just stopping in to pay my respects at Joe's suggestion. Fifteen minutes later she told me I was full of it: whether I knew it yet or not, I was destined to work for her. I just laughed it off, thinking "Lady, you've got a lot of nerve".

Four long one-on-one meetings later I was onboard as her Controller and Credit Manager. The closer was her success story, which began with a girl of 15 coming to the US alone as maid to a rich family in Forest Hills Gardens. She earned extra money mending and sewing on the side, and plowed it into a loop-ing machine, which meant more subcontract work, which meant another looping machine, and another, until she had a looping service, which quickly grew into a cut-and-sew sweater mill, which soon added onsite knitting machines, leaving her the owner of the largest knitting mill in Ridgewood, with more than 150 employ-ees and the costliest mansion in affluent Forest Hills Gardens. "Ed, I used to work for those people. Now I own the biggest house in the neighborhood."

She was happy to oblige me with a modest salary increase over my previous job, but as we shook hands she asked, "What are you going to do when your boss panics and offers you a lot more money?"

"We just shook hands. My handshake is my bond. See you in four weeks."

Feminine intelligence was vindicated again: Leo did indeed offer me substan-tially more when he saw he was losing me, and her question rang in my ears as I told him I had to turn him down.

Just after I started work in 1966, the mill closed down for the traditional Christmas break, but I stayed on the job to settle an IRS audit case before pro-duction resumed in mid-January. Anna called me into her office and chewed me out. "Don't you ever sell yourself short that way again!" Then she raised my salary above Leo's final offer. High marks indeed from my Gottscheer fairy godmother. It was the beginning of an exciting ride that would propel me to Executive Vice President, reporting to her son Joe when he took over as President.

You could not be point man even for a knitting mill in those days without encountering the Organization, since they controlled every "private sanitation" firm in New York City. When we bought a building abandoned 25 years earlier during its buildout as a movie theater, two sanitation companies started a territo-rial dispute over us as soon as our doors opened. Both sent invoices and I refused to pay either. When they started hijacking each other's containers and dumping the garbage in the street, I asked my friend Lou, who had his own garbage busi-ness, to intercede with the Don, and within two weeks one company's containers abruptly disappeared.

Unions were also in bed with the Organization and tried every year to orga-nize our workers, but our employee relations were so good that it never came to a vote. This did not stop my receptionist from summoning me into the factory lobby one day to confront two huge goons, one of whom announced, "Ai, ve is representing youse voikers."

Faking surprise: "When was the election? I musta been outa town." These were Teamster reps hustling illegal sweetheart deals with mill owners behind the employees' backs. For $9 per employee per month, plus sinecures for three goons, they would protect us from rival racketeers, at least until the cops found out and sent us all to the slammer.

"You can sign the papers now, or you can do it the hard way."

"Thanks very much, but I'll stick with the hard way." After I escorted them out a chill ran through me. Confronting wiseguys was the same at any age. Had I really tossed them out? Guys like that don't fool around, and here I was, not even the owner. Time to call the local precinct captain and explain we were in for a fight.

Two days later two men appeared in dark suits. When one of them introduced himself as Franky Dio I must have blanched both white and yellow: Johnny Dio was the president of the union, currently serving time in the federal pen for extortion. Franky cracked up as he handed me his ID: "I always get the same reaction." He was a detective with the Brooklyn Racketeering Squad; they just wanted to ask a few questions.

Everyday life became a special op. They shadowed me every night, and to throw them off the scent I had to head the wrong way home, through downtown Brooklyn, and ditch them on the Brooklyn Bridge. Several weeks of hellish tension later, the phone rang. "I wouldn't start that gray Buick tonight if I was you." Click. Time stood still as I opened the door and leaned halfway in to turn the ignition key at arm's length—a senseless precaution considering how little difference it would have made had there really been a bomb.

Their next stunt was hundreds of nails under my tires, every one of which had to go before it was safe to move in either direction. Then the climax, a live 30-millimeter shell on the hood of the Buick. It still lives in my office as a reminder of those unduly interesting times.

Six other Ridgewood mills were intimidated into signing up, but when the Feds busted the hoods to pieces we got to breathe deeply and pat ourselves on the back for standing our ground.

The stress may have been high, but the compensation kept pace: top salary, bonuses, a new company car every few years, annual vacations to Spain, Mexico, Barbados, Antigua. Any outsider would have sworn we were living the American Dream. One year we would visit Irmina's family in Germany, and the next her mother would spend months as our guest.

Irmina's pining for a European career was a thing of the past. Becoming an American citizen had meant the Good Life: expensive jewelry, new cars, modern furniture, everything affluent consumerism had to offer, including insatiability. True fulfillment was always one step ahead in the maze of desires. Perhaps she could catch up with it in the new bazaar of the Inner Self, the Human Potential Movement.

Human potential for me meant rounding the home stretch of my studies, just one year away from a college degree. Instead of a convenient subway ride downtown from my Manhattan office, night school had become a mad dash by car from Brooklyn through the Midtown Tunnel, down to Baruch College on 27th Street.

Manhattan parking is a religious ritual which gets old very fast when you are chronically half an hour late and out of breath after running up five flights. Modern city planners count on this frustration, and I decided to give them their way, simply taking the first available spot with or without fire hydrant and viewing the tickets as an education tax.

Graduating from the Baruch Division of the City College of New York in the Spring of 1968 with my Bachelor of Business Administration accounting major was another planetary leap in our family history. But it was inner space that drew Irmina, and the stage was set for us to diverge into parallel universes.

26

Through A Glass, Darkly

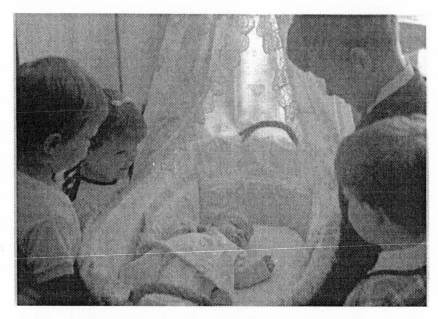

Steven, Sonya, baby David, Richie and Thomas, the cousins

Through A Glass, Darkly

Graduation had come just in time. Friedrich Knitting Mills had become number one in the industry, with 250 employees, and was still growing by leaps and bounds. We had purchased a large complex in Glendale to keep pace, and dealing with a 70000-square-foot facility left no room for night school.

The owners were happy to let me take on any duties that appealed to me, so I kept filling voids and suddenly found myself in charge not only of finances, fiscal and accounting but also manufacturing and marketing. Since no one else had the education or drive, I became Executive Vice President almost by default. Expansion meant sixteen departments reporting to the Executive VP, who reported direct to the President, Joe Friedrich, and the Chairman, Anna Friedrich.

Long gone were the days when Irmina needed to work. My income more than sufficed for a family, and behold, our second son appeared in April 1969. This time there was no argument about his name; "David Michael Stalzer" was perfect for the cutest redheaded baby possible.

Obscurity also became a thing of the past when I was listed that year in Who's Who in Finance and Industry, having earned the respect of the banking industry through my financial dealings as Vice President, but I was not content to rest on my laurels. Applying to Alexander Hamilton Institute, I was on my way to an MBA equivalent, the correspondence-school precursor of today's Open University and Internet degrees.

Nothing beats a case study you are involved in up to your neck every day, and this was the ideal synergy of theory and practice, but it did mean more time away from my family, so when it was done I took a two-year study hiatus. Steven had skipped kindergarten and gone straight to first grade when the nuns discovered he was already reading at first grade level and would be bored if held back. We had our doubts about the socialization implications but trusted their judgment and enrolled him at Our Lady of Mercy School in Forest Hills.

The result was a star grade-school pupil who went on to win several citywide science fairs, turning his Papa into his executive assistant. His ideas were so advanced that at one fair I was accused of doing the project for him, when in reality I barely understood what he was up to. He would come into my office, now less than ten minutes from home, and dictate his papers to me straight off the top of his head, outlining the project, its goals, his test results. Playing typist deep into the night was great fun and filled me with pride.

Gradually I broached the idea of my return to school, but Irmina was not keen, repeating her familiar accusations that I neglected her and the children "to bury my head in books". Really I had made it my business to study only after the children were in bed, and early in the morning, and there was still one more tool needed to complete my success toolbox. It came from a two-year correspondence course with the LaSalle Institute in mid-1973, which I finished in a record 18 months, earning an LLB in Business Law.

This was everything I needed to make it all the way to the top, but there would be a high cost in pain and suffering. Irmina was becoming more and more dissatisfied: raising kids was honorable but just not enough. Playing tennis while the kids were at school was not enough. Queens College was not enough. Only the meaning of life would do. She had to embark on a quest for the Holy Grail of the era, The Inner Self, Inner Peace.

The ensuing nightmare began innocently enough, with one of her routine calls to my office. Would I please come home early, she was going out for a meeting. What sort of meeting? Apparently a very exciting sort: "I found a notice in the paper about a bible study group that meets once a week in Jamaica. It's the ARE." What was the ARE? "The Association for Research and Enlightenment, an Edgar Cayce study group, you know, the prophet I have been reading about."

Come to think of it, those books had been popping up quite often. The most conspicuous were Thomas Sugrue's *There Is A River*, Jess Stearns' *The Sleeping Prophet*, Gina Cerminara's *Many Mansions*, and another Edgar Cayce biography whose author escapes me. Obviously I was going to need a handle on Edgar Cayce if I was to appreciate my wife's efforts.

On the surface he had started out quite an ordinary man, an accomplished photographer, father of two, gardener and Sunday School teacher. But he claimed that since childhood he had been able to read an entire book simply by lying on top of it when he went to sleep, and to recite it word for word upon awakening.

Lying down on a couch, the adult Cayce would allow himself to fall into a trance, an unusually relaxed, meditative sleep state where he answered questions from people all over the world as he lay upon their letters. Over forty years the stenographer recorded more than 14000 readings, the world's most extensive psychic database. The ARE was founded in Virginia Beach, Virginia in 1931 to catalog them and investigate the psychic realm.

On Cayce's death in 1945 the reins passed to his son Hugh Lynn, who grew ARE from a few hundred local members to tens of thousands worldwide before his death in 1982.

Bible study was what drew Irmina to ARE, but her interest in the readings metastasized until they dominated our family life, our religion, our dreams, health, parenting, business dealings. "Edgar Cayce said" was the final word on any subject covered in the readings, and the readings covered every cubic micrometer of the cosmos.

Dr. William Riley, a Cayce associate and author of a book on drug-free health, became our health and wellness guru. No need for pediatricians, just look up your child's illness in the index and buy what you are told.

Irmina was devoured by her new religion, poring over manuscripts day and night and offering our home as ARE's Northeast headquarters. No meaning in your life? Just drop in unannounced at the Stalzers'. She had found a mission as self-appointed spiritual leader, the true voice of Cayce.

When domestic life grew burdensome to the enlightened master, Hugh Lynn Cayce cautioned her that Cayce insisted on putting family first, but like those Christians who maintain Christ missed the point of the Old Testament and Revelation, Irmina dismissed the opinion of her supposed hero. She had seen the future in a dream. Family eggs would have to be broken for her gnostic omelette. The few must suffer so that she could minister to the desperate masses. And suffer they did: one convenient advantage of infinite wisdom, in peace as in war, is the ability to diagnose and punish thoughtcrime before it even enters the sublunary realm the vulgar call reality.

Tradition attempted to come to my aid; I turned the stumbling block into a veritable assembly line for stepping stones, engulfing myself in Cayce until I could argue either for or against as glibly as any lawyer in Manhattan. Joining a dream analysis group, I was instructed that all color dreams recalled past lives, where some failure had roped us into reincarnation. Either we got it right this time around the wheel or we would be right back in the mud of another physical existence.

The dread secret of my karma was that I had failed Irmina in several past lives and now existed for the sole purpose of underwriting her work. Quite an indictment, with the female id as prosecutor, judge, jury and—not executioner: apparently I did possess one tiny vein of virtue, having once saved her from being burned at the stake as a witch.

Sauce for the goose is sauce for the gander. I had seen a striking movie a few months earlier, and when my turn came to recite my dream, it happened to be in living color. I walked on the Pharaoh's right hand as we descended into a pyramid in long, stunning robes, dazzling gems bedecking our necks, our wrists, our headdress. At the bottom of the stairs was a large treasure chest overflowing with gold and precious stones. Suddenly we heard heavy steps and turned to discover a contingent of warriors advancing on us from above, arrows and spears at the ready, seemingly intent on robbery.

The Pharaoh's right hand index finger was in the air immediately, striking down the first row with a bolt of lightning, but one of the arrows found its mark and felled him. Whereupon I was shocked to watch my own finger dispatching the entire crew with the same lightning. I had succeeded the Pharaoh. Then I awoke in a cold sweat.

A color dream so vivid was irrefutable proof that I had once ruled Egypt, so from that day onward I was "the man". Belief in the essential rationality of humankind cannot long survive confrontation with this level of gullibility, its instant reverence for self-proclaimed psychics and healers. Irmina became the pivot of their lives, dispensing endless hours of wisdom to those trapped in marriages less perfect than hers. Our house became a magnet for neurotics. If I got home late, as I did most every night, I was under orders to tiptoe into the basement and remain below in silence, while our children remained mute in their rooms, until audible movement upstairs marked the end of group meditation. Only then could I share the free dinner that inevitably awaited my wife's guests.

Finally even the basement was no longer safe; one night I returned to find it transformed into a lecture room where a beaming Irmina introduced me to a "famous psychic" from Columbus, Ohio. How very lucky we were that this august personage had deigned to present her findings in our humble dwelling. Ignoring such an honor would have been most uncouth, and as they began chanting their mantra I did my husbandly best, slipping into my deepest basso profundo and pretending to meditate: Om, Om. Satchinananda, here I come.

Following this holiday from materialism, the psychic graciously accepted voluntary donations, deftly whisking banknotes into her brassiere. Later on, as she was checking out the take in the dining room, some mischievous gremlin decided to send me in as a witness to her occult verdict: "Those cheap bastards!"

Instead of cringing in mortification, the lady was a cool enough customer to speculate that her overnight host might yet be persuaded to believe her rather than his own eyes. She treated her disgrace as an opportunity to flatter me on my superb chanting voice, urging me to join her on the living room floor for psychic intimacy.

We adopted the easy lotus position, face to face, and she took my hands in hers, inviting me to meditate as she entered her trance, straining my courtesy with her ludicrous "out-of-the-body" voice.

Channeling my vital statistics to the spirits, she received the bulletin that I was charitable, kind, spiritual, giving. An honest soul.

"And unbelievably handsome".

"Shut up, Ed, concentrate." She tried to resume the trance pose, but the spell was broken: I burst out laughing, and so did she. This was no fool; she knew who was feeding her that weekend. We wandered along to the nightly banquet, which that night was followed by a hands-on healing session. Everyone in the circle closed his eyes, meditated and laid hands on the person in front, supposedly to transfer healing energy. Call me wishful, but I played right along, praying Irmina would eventually perceive the folly of it all. No such luck; it encouraged her more every time.

Our psychic had heard so much about Brooklyn and wanted so badly to see it; could she impose upon me to give her a tour that very night? Soon I was dutifully driving her across the Brooklyn Bridge, where somehow I took a wrong turn and landed at the dark and empty docks. Menacing homeless men had sought shelter there, and her face shifted into its psychic expression: "I have a feeling we should leave this place immediately."

"No sh-t, Dick Tracy, you don't have to be psychic to get that message". At least she took it with humor as we beat our hasty retreat.

By now I had read enough to pull my weight at the discussions. Parts of my skepticism were too strong to conceal or mute, and my refusal to buy into reincarnation piqued Irmina particularly. "If you can't agree with Cayce's theories, can't you at least keep quiet and not embarrass me?" Yet the more original texts I read, the clearer it became that most of Cayce's teachings were just not that far off the beaten track: routine Judeo-Christian doctrine, updated Old Testament. The bizarre flowers grew mainly in the minds of his interpreters.

Occasional visits with Irmina to Virginia Beach confirmed this impression. Hugh Lynn Cayce was a dedicated psychologist sincere in the beliefs inherited from his father. The same went for most of the staff. Hugh Lynn enjoyed getting a skeptical workout, and he respected me for keeping an open mind, but he never proselytized. He did invite me to participate in the ARE's annual management conference, correctly suspecting I might enjoy analyzing some of Cayce's reflections on business. After three days immersed in readings I agreed to write a short post-conference article for the ARE newsletter, part of which read:

> **To me, the highlight of the entire weekend was the research project, requiring each of us to research the readings related to business. We shared our knowledge in group reports given on Sunday morning, summarizing what we had learned. Every report given, whether on the subject of big or small business, manufacturing, profit, advertising, selling or per-**

sonnel, appeared to say the same thing: SERVICE. This concept can best be described by quotes from Reading #1634-1:

"Then, have that policy to do unto others as ye would have others do to you. EXPECT that! LIVE that in thy dealings! And ye will find that He who is the Giver of all good and perfect gifts will bring to thy experience not only harmony and peace, but greater opportunities, with material, social and financial success."

"If thy purposes are ALONE for self-aggrandizement, the gaining for self only of a monetary return, then ye may find that others will consider same in the same manner and act in the same manner."

On that note we parted company, much wiser, many of us with new ideals, some of us with old ideals reinforced, but all of us very grateful for having had the opportunity to share this conference with each other.

The ARE would have been fine if only Irmina had practiced what they preach rather than branching out into unrelated supernatural areas. Cayce was not responsible for the Hindu altar which appeared in the living room of our Catholic home. The neighbors threw a fit when she called in her guru and a cast of dozens for a spectacularly colorful ecumenical ceremony.

Not long thereafter she announced she was taking the boys to ARE summer camp in Rural Retreat, Virginia; I could join them or not as I pleased. Having overdosed on camping earlier in life, I had vowed never to do it again now that I could afford pleasant resorts, but I knew that if I stayed home they might well return brainwashed.

Camp was a rude awakening for the boys and Irmina, who might have known better given her evacuation drill in Germany. Upon arrival we were assigned a screened lean-to with another family; our sleeping bags rested on beds nailed together from logs and branches. The communal baths were in a log cabin several hundred yards into the woods. Vegetarian food, and chicken once a week, was served "family-style" in a large mess hall. And guess where we had to go to relieve ourselves. A latrine. A communal latrine, with holes for five people to sit and debate public policy. You could only go inside if the dial outside the door indicated the current occupants belonged to your own sex. Cleaning and deodorizing the latrines alternated on the duty roster with kitchen duty, gardening, and clearing tables.

So this was the good life I had worked so hard for: a return to refugee camp. What a hoot.

To be fair, there were also New Age activities and classes from morning until night: Cayce readings and Transcendental Meditation, nature hikes, acupuncture and drugless therapy, a trip to the watering hole, dream and Bible studies, pleasant evening singalongs. I fell into step and tried to convince the boys, who hated it all, that they were having fun experiencing nature. Anticipating vegetarian food, I had smuggled in some salami, which I shared with them in the woods when no one was looking.

The caving expedition reversed our roles. My childhood brushes with cave disaster still echoed faintly, and I let the boys go only on condition I would be along to help. The caves were just wide enough to slither through on one's stomach. The guide crawled in first, then Steven and David, with me holding up the rear. A stream trickling along the cave bed drenched our fronts before we were ten feet into the pitch blackness. This guide had better know what he was doing. One narrow pass almost wedged my hips in, but his voice led us through to a large cavern where we could rest. He had obviously done this many times, but my nerves stayed on edge.

The exit was a sudden sliver of light opening onto a vigorous stream that washed off the sand and mud. All of a sudden the kids did not need to be told they were having fun experiencing nature; they were hot to do it again the next day. Fortunately I could honestly remind them we had signed up for a mountain hike.

Any hope that camp might quench Irmina's occult thirst came to naught. She developed a bizarre obsession with automatic writing, explaining that her latest spirit guide entered her to guide her hand during trance. She often spent the whole night generating piles of scribblings to interpret for us. Invariably the guide instructed us to mend our ways and follow orders we had myopically resisted when Irmina issued them in the waking state.

The stale and tired concepts of reason and evidence finally capitulated altogether as she initiated us into the glorious future of science: the dowsing revolution. The art of dowsing became our philosopher's stone, indispensable whether we faced business problems, schooling decisions, or movie choices.

Dowsing is more than just the forked stick earlier generations used to 'witch' for water; the idea is to trick your unconscious into revealing its hidden wishes by letting your hand move 'by itself'. People use L-rods, Y-rods, bobbers, aurometers, probably knives and forks. Irmina's tool was the pendulum.

Personally I just cannot swallow this theory of accessing the unconscious. Guys like me need our theories testable, and nothing can ever really falsify claims of links between the pendulum and the unconscious. Even if you loosen up and allow for an occasional useful tip from the pendulum, there is a world of facts out there and you are embracing solipsism if you just assert that your unconscious controls them all.

Me, I review my facts, draw up my plan, and execute. With Irmina insisting I put everything on hold pending a dowsing decision, something was bound to give. When I tried to reason with her about constantly staying out after midnight, never being there to welcome the kids home from school, heading off to Virginia Beach all the time, her stock answer became "If you don't like it, move out." Old friends and family too had fallen by the way as her alien circle practically took up residence in our house.

My refuge from the tension was the Lake George cottage we had originally purchased in 1974 as a summer getaway. To protect the boys from overexposure to the occult, I took all my vacation time in the form of long-weekend days with them, fishing, swimming, mountain climbing, buying a 20-foot Sea Ray and making respectable sailors and waterskiers of ourselves. Mom was too busy for such frivolities; New York City alone still contained millions in need of a good lecturing.

27

Paradise Lost

The last family picture taken at the end of the school year 1982

Paradise Lost

Despite my habitual insistence that Mom just had a temporary problem, reviving domestic happiness was becoming Mission Impossible. All that remained was a rear guard action, spending as much time as possible with the kids to ensure they remained indifferent toward the ARE and the occult. "For better or for worse" was going under. Finally I had come up against a stumbling block that kept growing until it became a ten-foot wall. This case demanded not a steppingstone but a tall ladder.

The irony was that we had never looked more like the American Dream. A beautiful mother, two great kids with great grades, two cars, two houses, frequent vacations, private German and piano lessons for the boys—how much more could a superficial observer require?

Steven did tend to attract bullies. His fellow German student Walter constantly poked him in the back with a pencil, and one night I stepped in after class and put an end to it. "Hi, Walter, how's it going?" He looked as if he had been struck by lightning: his victim's parent knew his name. He got home to find me parked in front of his house. "Hi, Walter, how's it going?" His address too was no secret to the agent of divine retribution. Steven had no further problems with Walter.

Mind games are my specialty, but psychological warfare is not always enough. When a certain Johnny gave Steven eleven conspicuous arm bruises for his birthday, he came home for lunch and refused to go back to school. It was not the first time I had interrupted a supervisors' meeting and raced to the house. Steven had told me about this kid, and for a month I had been training him in self-defense. I reminded him there would have to be a showdown sooner or later.

As I dropped him back at school, he had scarcely left the car when Johnny jumped him and hurled him within inches of an oncoming car. I lost it, springing out and chasing the kid past the door monitor, into the school, and up two flights of stairs, catching him in the hall. When the nuns came running I explained I was not going to hurt Johnny, but I did have them bring me to Steven.

"OK, Steven, I now give you permission to beat the crap out of this guy.—Sister, I will be responsible." Off I strode in high dudgeon. Irmina went to pick Steven up that day and found him under teacher guard in the schoolyard, where he had struck back and creamed Johnny. The bully had met his match and Steven had learned never to tolerate harassment again. My final caution was never to let his newfound power go to his head, lest he become a bully himself.

David, being five years younger than Steven, was even more vulnerable to our troubles. This made for a special bond that kept me "tuned in" to him in a way that might have interested Irmina if she had been paying closer attention: she would have called it a sixth sense. Over the years there were many instances where one of us would blurt out what was on the tip of the other's tongue, making us both burst out laughing.

One afternoon he had gone to play with the other kids around the block when I got an overwhelming urge to drive over and check up on him. I arrived just as one of his classmates was about to beat him up. "Hey, David, need a ride?"

"How did you know I was hoping you'd come by?"

"Oh, I just had a feeling—"

Such moments were nearly extinct by the spring of 1982, when the nightmare of failed marriage finally forced me to grab the ladder and scale that ten-foot wall. Steven was in the final lap of highschool, 18 years old and college bound, old enough to call his own shots. David was about to graduate from grammar school and head off to St. Francis Catholic School; the judge found him mature enough at 13 to know his own interests when he chose paternal custody.

The mental anguish of midlife divorce proved even greater than the stresses of refugee childhood. Adult memory knows how to augment suffering with tormenting tatters of happier times and brighter hopes. Renouncing all worldly goods in exchange for custody was a body blow, but rumination was an Iron Maiden. What had become of the two young lovers who plighted their eternal troth? How had the satanic moment of no return slithered by unsuspected?

Starting all over again at Ground Zero meant a whole range of stumbling blocks: one son in college, another in school, voluntary alimony to Irmina, all amid the long goodbye to youth. But my father too had landed in America very close to the age of 43, with three mouths to feed from an empty pocket, and nothing was going to stop me from regaining my life as he had.

Settling in to fight the good fight, I promptly received my reminder that fate regards misfortune as a signal to attack. Anna Friedrich died of a massive heart attack at 62, and the heirs to her knitting mill were determined to disregard the advice of the man who had spent sixteen years of his life building their company into an industry leader. Certainly I had been compensated very fairly in good years and bad, but that was then. Now could not have looked much more like the end of the line for Ed Stalzer.

Time to pull out my entrepreneur's creed once more. "You've got to be willing to hang on a cliff 100 times, 200 times…be able to get knocked off and climb back up." That's me. Failure is not an option.

Twenty years in the trenches had molded me into quite a respectable business executive. Every venture I had touched had benefited from my unusual mix of expertise in accounting, finance, manufacturing, law, labor relations, general management. I had transformed a family business into a streamlined corporation with sixteen departments reporting to me, I had kept the Organization at bay, I had designed and developed the first ABS or Apparel Business System in collaboration with IBM.

All this won me a position as Chief Operating Officer of a sweater manufacturer, lasting until my divorce was granted in 1984 after almost 25 years of marriage. Steven was at Oberlin, David was living with his bachelor father, and at 45 I found myself "single with children". Never again would I get married. I had paid my dues.

Two years later both my sons graduated. David was already piloting small aircraft, and he flew off to Embry Riddle in Daytona Beach, Florida to pursue his dream of a commercial aviation career. After a year of freelance computer software development in Boston, Steven made it into Harvard and won his Master's in Education; he would end up a senior software engineer for Nokia, and he and his wife Valerie would eventually present me with my first granddaughter, Rosa Concetta Stalzer.

What more could a grateful father hope for in his sons, particularly considering the turmoil they had lived through? They were the phoenix, risen from the ashes of a dead love.

28

Bits And Pieces

Bits And Pieces

Seven lean years of confirmed bachelorhood were to come before my financial house was in order again; at one point I had maxed out a dozen credit cards just to cope with tuition. Though I dated a nice Irish lady, permanent relationships were too risky even to consider.

I had plunged into business for myself as a roving Chief Financial Officer for smaller sweater manufacturers. Some were excellent technicians but babes in the financial woods. Others had inherited a business they knew nothing about. Both needed me badly but could not afford me full time, so I offered my services on a per diem. My motto, needless to say, was "Let me turn your stumbling blocks into stepping stones".

From the start the demand was so great that I had no time for myself. One day a week here, two a month there, and pretty soon I was CFO for a dozen small companies in Brooklyn and Queens. Each agreed I could accept calls from any of the others so long as they too could track me down 24 hours a day. This arrangement kept me well in the loop but it did yield its share of comic opera. When a client called on my "bag phone" to tell me the bank needed some information, I would pull their latest financial report out of my magic briefcase and the bank would get a call from my home office, or one of my many branch offices such as LaGuardia or Central Park: "This is Ed Stalzer, CFO of Whichever Corporation, what can I do for you?"

My chance to "practice what I preached" came when the 74-year-old owner of a small sweater factory decided to get out of the business, also after a heart attack, and I bought his mill. Creating up to 65 jobs gave me the gratifying sensation of helping up to 65 deserving families, while earning a fantastic living.

The one sour note was a group of three brothers determined to rape a very successful mill they had inherited from their father, a man of legendary integrity. They cheated their employees out of overtime, stole from their customers. Their disreputability and personal extravagance grew notorious and pulled them toward the financial abyss.

Enter Edwin Stalzer Associates, the wizard at extricating financially tangled firms. The City of New York had a loan subsidy and guarantee program aimed at companies impacted by imports, and their father had built just such a company. If I could convince a bank to lend to them, the city would cosign, but first the company had to be reorganized, with less fanciful financial statements. It took months, and reams of paperwork, but the bank came on board and after due review the City decided to join them.

Just one twist: the agreement called for Edwin Stalzer to continue as consultant until the half a million dollars was repaid. To ensure repayment, a half-million-dollar insurance policy would be taken out on Edwin Stalzer.

The City was asking me to put my life on the line for three bums who just the month before had forced me to veto the liquidation of their widowed mother's home. Should they ever get the impulse to walk away from their responsibilities, they would need only invest $2000 in one of Brooklyn's many unemployed hit men.

So the answer was no. Pleading, and eventual threats, did not alter my decision. The City pulled the offer and the mill went down the tubes.

They were the only Stalzer Associates clients to fail. The rest of the story was industry-wide recognition, speaking engagements, invitations to attend conventions and contribute articles to the industry magazine, "The Bobbin". Single-minded Gottscheer devotion to the task at hand had freed me like Houdini from the financial straitjacket.

29

Soulmate

Ed and Carol

Soulmate

Life can be so perverse that it is hard to tell which amuses it more: levying hidden taxes on ambition, or randomly showering us with blessings we have honestly renounced. Now that gathering rosebuds was the very last thing on my mind, it started winking at me, popping up on the client lists of Edwin Stalzer Associates companies under the ironic alias of Garland Industries.

Garland stood out against the rough-and-tumble background of the rag trade, where it can be so crucial to screen your associates twice. Self-evident professionalism became the norm when you crossed paths with their technical director, Carol Smith, who farmed out their excess production and monitored the subcontractors.

One day I was working in the back office of one of the mills when I heard an altercation on the factory floor. The two owners and their forelady were out there haranguing Carol, refusing to replace incorrect labels they had already sewn into thousands of sweaters, angrily insisting Garland had supplied the wrong labels.

Sheer idiocy. Regardless of blame, you never shout at customers and you never nix their requests outright. "Pack up the garments and ship them to my place, I'll do the job free of charge." When the day ended they were locked in at my mill with Carol, who proceeded personally to remove every label. By 11am the next morning a crew of my ladies had completed production on time and we had saved the day.

Helping a colleague out of a jam paid multiple dividends. Carol started not only channeling regular work into my mill but also drastically upgrading our overall standards through the example of her quality control. Seeing her more often also suited my personal fancy. Nothing could ever come of it: she was as demure as she was fashionable, and her wedding ring reminded the likes of me to keep our admiration at an appropriate distance. But I secretly enjoyed watching her walk off in her tight little leather skirts and jewelry and furs, as I pretended not to notice. I wondered at first how she could cut such a figure in these sleazy neighborhoods without getting mugged. The trick was that the pimps and prostitutes she walked past between mills figured only a sting operator with NYPD backup could be so blithely oblivious to the obvious risks.

We found ourselves working at another mill one midday, and taking a deep breath, I casually mentioned I was headed over to Gebhard's for lunch. Would she care to join me? Surprisingly enough, yes.

Two hours spent exchanging life stories over German food revealed we had plenty in common, beginning with reluctance to toss the dice of marriage again after a lamentable failure. Her wedding ring had stayed on after divorce just to ward people off. She had married her highschool sweetheart and swiftly descended into a 17-year pit of mental cruelty and financial instability.

That lunch was the inauguration of a perfect friendship. On the surface we were polar opposites, I the motormouth extrovert and she the consummate introvert, but the more time we spent together enjoying tennis and the theater, the more obvious our complementarity became. Deep down we had the same outlook and ultimate goals, so she naturally supported everything I did, helping me in my work at every turn. Being so much in synch was an uncanny novelty. How could an adult relationship run on autopilot? Where was the knife fight?

God forbid I should ever marry again, but if that calamity should descend, Carol would surely minimize the damage. How jejune and rash I had been as a bridegroom of twenty, when I really needed the calm analysis maturity had made second nature. Carol's entries lined up of their own accord on the asset side of the ledger: tons of common interests, unattached, relatively youthful, successful, no golddigging, no children to renew the college tuition burden after David finished in two years, no annoying traits to rationalize away until it was too late. Not one dealbreaker.

The boys sensed it too. She had met David a few times after school and they hit it off right away. They could relate as friends, free of parental overtones, and David began confiding more personally in her than in me. Steven had not seen her so often but they also got along fine.

The deal was win-win from every angle: no one demanded anything from anyone else, so being together was a plus without a minus. A rose without a thorn. Wait a minute, Plato said the chances of finding our other half were next to nil once the gods chopped us in two for our hubris and shuffled the deck. Could it really be that I had won the soulmate lottery without even buying a ticket? Beam me up, Scotty, I think I'm falling...

For my fiftieth birthday I threw a big bash for fifty friends at the local German restaurant and introduced Carol to the whole gang. She got a double thumbs up from everyone including my parents and Richie. Some speculated that the game was afoot, but I played it close to my chest. Only the boys could be fairly certain I had an arrow through my heart: why else would I have floated the notion of remarriage?

Sure, Dad, go for it. Very well, I would marry my soulmate, albeit thirty years too late. There was of course the not-so-minor detail of her consent. My proposal was far from the controlless core of youthful romance. And was remarriage an idea she could even entertain? "Probably, if it was somebody like you, somebody I could rely on."

Wow, that was easy enough. "Well, then, would you do me the honor of becoming my wife?"

Not a blockbuster movie scene, perhaps, but eminently practical and down to earth. We discussed it like any other project. How would it play with our families? What was the downside? There was no reason not to do it, because we already had the magic ingredient many marriages never find: we were best friends, acting out our own agenda rather than letting the genes hijack our reason for their own ends. If people concentrated on being friends first and lovers second, the divorce rate would plummet.

The perfect friendship became the perfect merger three days after Carol's fortieth birthday, with Steven and David as joint best men. There had been a discreet civil ceremony in Kew Gardens Court a few days earlier, but though we were divorced Catholics who wanted our second marriage to make as little splash as possible, we did want an official church wedding with guests. The pastor at the beautiful nondenominational church in Forest Hills Gardens was delighted to oblige. Friends and family joined us for the service and the subdued reception at a Forest Hills restaurant, delighted to toast our second chance at life.

Our partnership has succeeded beyond our fondest hopes in every aspect of our lives. When David needed special courses, Carol volunteered as banker and saw David through to graduation from Embry Riddle, on his way to being a 767 pilot for United.

30

Karl May's America

My first horse, a Karl May dream come true

Karl May's America

New York City was our professional habitat, Carol as a designer and sample-room supervisor, I as consultant and mill owner. But on our vacations we kept an eye out for the ideal retirement niche. The truth was that by 1992 we were over-dosing on New York. I had not forgotten the noble savage, and Carol was convinced she would get a call someday informing her I had been shot or knifed.

What worried her was that, for better or for worse, I have never been able to resist interfering with crimes in progress. Some of my impromptu police risks are hard to explain rationally; they must strike childhood chords from partisans and bullies. Once when I witnessed a Brooklyn mugging I jumped out of my car and nailed the mugger, literally sitting on him until the police came, surrounded by a dozen sympathetic Hispanics. The victim had run away, leaving me without a witness, so it was lucky they took my side and helped hem him in until the police arrived.

Why did these macho stunts continue at my age? Why did I rip Magic Markers and spray cans from the hands of graffiti vandals tall enough for professional basketball?

The climax of my avenger career began with a stroll up Seventh Avenue on the way to a Broadway show. By the time my nerves ferried, processed and returned the information about a slap on my right side, a pickpocket had cleaned out my pants pocket. I dropped my shopping bag and dashed off in pursuit, a hotheaded move for someone proud of being streetwise. I was on his tail heading east on 45th to Broadway, then way down south. The instant before I nabbed him he darted across 34th Street and disappeared into Macy's.

Only then did it hit me: the old trick of decoying the husband so your partner can steal the wife's diamonds. I flagged down a police cruiser and they called colleagues cruising the neighborhood where I had abandoned Carol. When they drove her up ten minutes later she was greatly relieved I had not caught the thief. $150 was cheap insurance. What if he had put a knife in my belly? What if I had killed him? What if he had had the gall to claim I was the one stealing from him? The voice of reason sounded hostile at first, but grew friendlier the closer my heartrate sank toward normality.

Between the pages of "International Living" there existed a world free of such random shocks, sparkling with the lively indolence of retirement. One playmate of the month was Charlottesville, Virginia, home of Thomas Jefferson and the University of Virginia; the patriotism gave me goose bumps. We drove to Charlottesville for the Labor Day weekend, staying at the Clifton Inn where Jefferson's daughter lived, following up all the magazine's leads: Jefferson's home at Monti-cello, James Madison's at Ash Lawn, UVA, lots of area horse farms.

Here it was, patiently waiting, the America I had dreamed of as a boy reading Karl May. Farms, rolling hills, rivers, the Blue Ridge Mountains as backdrop. All my old dreams came flooding back, together with a new conviction. This was where we were going to retire. So certain were we that we bought a building lot in a golfing community. Finally I was going to have my own horse.

Retirement age was still far off and we did not yet have the money we needed, so figuring out how to get to Charlottesville became our top priority. In 1995 the gears clicked into place: the house was finished, our New York business sold, and I became CEO and part-owner of Virginia Electronic Components, in business since 1949.

It had taken 43 years to find the country Karl May revealed to me in 1948 at Camp 7, but riding my horse up into the Virginia mountains I knew the journey had reached its destination, the true American Dream.

31

Full Circle

Ed at the former site of Camp #5 with old "Bohler Werke" in background
June 17, 2001. In 1945 this fence was 8-10 feet high topped by barbed
wire.

Full Circle

Fifty years had passed since last I set foot on Austrian soil; the refugee camps had long since been replaced by industrial parks and subdivisions. Had any traces of those ancient lives withstood the lapping tides of time?

The general desire to show Carol my roots had become specific on visits to my cousin Elfie and her husband Joe in Atlanta. Elfie was a few years younger, so her memories were less vivid, more in need of external stimulation. I welcomed her nudge and we took off from Washington Dulles for Munich in 2001, driving a rental down to Salzburg.

For the first week of the trip we played tourist, partly ignoring the ghosts that roam those mountains. Schladming, fifty miles south of Salzburg, was one of Austria's busiest winter ski resorts, a perfect base for exploring the countryside in the off season, and the Alps right outside our hotel made the stop feel like *The Sound of Music* rather than an opening skirmish with the spirits of our own past.

Heading south through Klagenfurt, with its monument to the Gottscheers, we returned to Graz, just a few miles from the Slovenian border, and hunted for hints of the city we had entered on foot in 1945. Only the Turm remained, though at the top of its steps we did find a monument dedicated to the city by thankful refugees.

At Bruck an der Mur the trail went hot. Behind the hotel desk was a young lady named Kristina; as she checked us in we chatted and I told her that in another lifetime I had been a student at the Hauptschule in Kapfenberg, a refugee from one of the nearby camps.

"Oh, my God!" she exclaimed, "were you in Camp 5?" Yes. "Are you from Yugoslavia?" Yes again. "You must be a Gottscheer." I certainly am. "Oh, my God, oh, my God, excuse me, I must call my mother."

She arranged for us to meet her family the next morning at Sunday Mass down the road in Mürzzuschlag, and we hardly slept that night. The Röthel family met us with open arms: father, mother, two daughters, one daughter-in-law and one grandchild. After Mass they invited us to the parish hall farewell dinner for their priest, and we could not stop talking.

Kristina's parents were not only Gottscheers but also members of the wagon train out of Königsberg. Unbeknownst to us, they had been our neighbors in Camp 5 for seven years, electing to live out the rest of their lives in nearby Marein. This sealed the permanent bond of friendship, and we vowed to spend a month in Kapfenberg every year once we became full-time grandparents and I a part-time CEO.

The dam had broken, and the stream of childhood associations burst its banks. Taking our leave, we drove straight up to Lorenzen. "Turn right at the church, then take an immediate left. There used to be a little stream there. Then we have to drive up the valley." Here civilization had not blemished the tranquility of memory. Even the anonymous caves of our boyhood expeditions remained intact. Like a long-lost friend granted surreal exemption from old age, the chapel still stood atop the hill where we had so often harvested raspberries.

Camp 5 itself had morphed into an industrial park, but the next morning we found the environs still so full of clues that I needed only stand at the new fence and close my eyes to call forth the world of my younger self, the self of barracks and scavenging, in the vivid color of an actual past life. Imagination could almost revivify even the sounds and scents. There was our skiing hill, and there the factory buildings on the right. The atmosphere of my Confirmation and First Communion still permeated the rundown interior of the chapel across the street. Gasthaus Stieglbauer was serving lunch, and its owner Franz Stieglbauer, born in 1945, had written his own comprehensive chronicle of the camp; a signed copy sits proudly on our library shelf.

Marein too was there to greet its erstwhile foundling. The churches stood firm with their eternal message; renovation had not changed the outlines of the Volksschule; the railway station awaited some other boy covertly covering his homework overdraft; even the movie house testified to the stolen delights of our Johnny Weissmueller days. Franz Schichtler had lived on at 9 Main Street after his parents' death and become an engineer. How I wish he had lived a few years longer, to share in the vindication of our boyhood Karl May reveries, perhaps even to accompany me someday on an odyssey through Slovenia, all the way back to the land of Gottschee.

The thought of so much revelation at once must have overtaxed the modesty of the past. She closed the museum before I could determine the fate of the enchanted sword I had once traded for the fine gold of manhood; and when we entered the school, though my former math classroom was open, June had melted away the graceful gliding ski-jumpers, and the boys and Pythagoras and Oxford English. Or were they still hovering round about us in some other realm? We exchanged smiles with the janitors as we walked out into the fresh breeze.

Afterword

Edwin Stalzer and his wife Carol continue to live the American Dream in Charlottesville, Virginia, the home of Thomas Jefferson. They live in a spacious home built along a golf course in a gated community. Horseback riding, tennis, golf are frequent diversions, as well as long walks around the numerous paths on the property.

Although he is still managing two businesses, Ed has made good on his promise to "slow down" and spend more time away from the office after turning 65 in May of 2004.

Carol and Ed travel extensively to New York City and Boston to visit family and are finally exploring the rest of the United States and Europe. In 2005 they are planning to travel to Slovenia for the first time since 1945 to attempt to find the ruins of Ed's family home in Gottschee and to retrace the refugee exodus from Gottschee to Austria.

APPENDIX A

The author most gratefully acknowledges the Gottscheer organizations and authors whose historical work helped him better understand the meaning of Gottschee through the centuries. Among these are:

- The Gottscheer Hilfswerk or Gottscheer Relief Association of Ridgewood, New York

- The Gottscheer Organization of Klagenfurt, Austria, publishers of "650 Jahre Gottschee—Festbuch 1980" (Celebrating 650 Years of Gottschee)

- Herman Petschauer, compiler of "Das Jahrhundert Buch", translated by Herma Moschner as "Gottschee and Its People Through the Centuries" and published by the Gottscheer Relief Association in 1984

- Gottschee.com and gottschee.org

- "GOTTSCHEE The Resettlement Years" by Edeltraud M. Krauland, Pioneer Publishing

APPENDIX B

Picture Gallery

Joseffa Stalzer (1871-1933)   Eustachius Stalzer (1869-1931)

Rosa and Adolf Stalzer

Andreas and Josefa Pitzel

First Holy Communion

Aunt Ida's house in Ridgewood

Richard, Mama, Papa and Edwin
Smithtown, (1952)

My buddy, Ben Budelmann

Benny, Joan and Helen Budelmann (1952)

Growing up in Brooklyn

My parents, Rosa and Adolf
Their 4 family house in Ridgewood, circa 1964

My First Love 1955–1957

Senior Prom

"Little Nato" meeting

On Maneuvers—1958

David's Christening

Graduations
Steven—Harvard
David—Embry Riddle

Captain David Stalzer

Wedding Day—Nov. 25, 1989

"Full Circle"
Trip to Austria June 2001